Phonetics, Phonology & Pronunciation for the Language Classroom

Phonetics, Phonology & Pronunciation for the Language Classroom

Charles Hall
Alfaisal University, Saudi Arabia

Christopher Hastings
US State Department English Language Fellow, ITMO University, Russia

Applied Linguistics for the Language Classroom
Series Editor: Andy Curtis

BLOOMSBURY ACADEMIC
LONDON • NEW YORK • OXFORD • NEW DELHI • SYDNEY

BLOOMSBURY ACADEMIC
Bloomsbury Publishing Plc
50 Bedford Square, London, WC1B 3DP, UK
1385 Broadway, New York, NY 10018, USA
29 Earlsfort Terrace, Dublin 2, Ireland

BLOOMSBURY, BLOOMSBURY ACADEMIC and the Diana logo
are trademarks of Bloomsbury Publishing Plc

First published 2017 by PALGRAVE

Reprinted by Bloomsbury Academic

Copyright © 2017 Charles Hall and Christopher Hastings

Charles Hall and Christopher Hastings have asserted their rights under the Copyright, Designs and Patents Act, 1988, to be identified as the authors of this work.

For legal purposes the Acknowledgements on p. xvii-xviii constitute an extension of this copyright page.

All rights reserved. No part of this publication may be reproduced or transmitted in any form or by any means, electronic or mechanical, including photocopying, recording, or any information storage or retrieval system, without prior permission in writing from the publishers.

Bloomsbury Publishing Plc does not have any control over, or responsibility for, any third-party websites referred to or in this book. All internet addresses given in this book were correct at the time of going to press. The author and publisher regret any inconvenience caused if addresses have changed or sites have ceased to exist, but can accept no responsibility for any such changes.

A catalogue record for this book is available from the British Library.

A catalog record for this book is available from the Library of Congress.

ISBN: PB: 978-1-1375-5468-0
ePDF: 978-1-1375-5467-3

To find out more about our authors and books visit
www.bloomsbury.com and sign up for our newsletters.

For Josephine, Stefan, and the future

Contents

List of Figures and Tables viii
Preface ix
Series Editor's Introduction xiii
Acknowledgements xvii

1 Introduction 1
2 Phonetics 16
3 Phonology 74
4 Research and Pronunciation 101
5 Syllables and Suprasegmentals 127
6 Language Varieties & English as a Lingua Franca 154
7 Technology and Pronunciation Teaching 167
8 Conclusion 180

Glossary 186
References 195
Index 201

List of Figures and Tables

Figures

2.1	Cross-section of head	21
2.2	Basic vowel chart	49
2.3	Venn diagram of front vowels	62
2.4	American English vowel chart	67

Tables

2.1	English bilabial consonants	24
2.2	Interdental fricatives	28
2.3	Descriptions of front vowels	61
2.4	Descriptions of back vowels	65
2.5	Descriptions of American English vowels	67
3.1	Chinese phonotactics and english syllables	98
6.1	EFL and ELF pronunciation targets	162

Preface

This book began as a discussion – a conversation that began more than a decade before any work on this book – between a professor and his student, both of whom are students of language. The professor was educated in theoretical linguistics (specializing in diachronic syntax) in the 1970s, but earned his way teaching English as a Second Language (ESL), English as a Foreign Language (EFL) and German. His teaching career began in 1972 as language teachers were making the shift away from behaviourist models of teaching and looking towards what would become known Communicative Language Teaching (CLT). After earning a business degree, the student began his studies in linguistics long after CLT had become dominant in English language teaching, and his education almost entirely focused on the practical application of theory in the classroom. Although his foreign language classes were most frequently taught using outdated pedagogical models ranging from grammar translation to no theory at all, he was taught to teach English with communication as the main focus. Unfortunately, in this model, some of the theory was de-prioritized, and there was a separation between his classroom practice and the theory on which it is founded. As such, this book was created out of the dialogue that emerged as the professor attempted to explain theoretical issues to his student. Now we are both professors, and the first professor is proud to say that the student has become a great teacher and helps his professor understand much of the world. Teacher and student are, after all, often just arbitrary titles in the learning-centred life.

Before beginning work on each section of the book, we began by exploring the issues with a discussion of how each of the topics had been introduced to us in our respective school experiences or the many foreign language classes we took. We next considered how this knowledge served (or didn't serve) us when we got into the language classroom and began teaching for ourselves. The differences between our backgrounds were almost immediately apparent, with one of us having to take the theory he had learned and adapt it to put it to some practical use and the other having to take the practice he had learned and supplement it with further study into the underlying theory of his pedagogy.

In discussing these issues with our colleagues, we discovered what is also visible in the literature, namely that one of the casualties of the CLT revolution was a focus on pronunciation teaching. So many CLT professionals simply assumed that pronunciation was either unimportant or would fend for itself. On the other hand, as a student in a secondary boys school in Hamburg, Germany, the professor continued his own foreign/second language learning with the conviction that a 'native' accent was an ideal target for language learners. As a result, he knew that his German and French teachers in the 1960s and early 1970s needed a solid grounding in articulatory phonetics, the production of different speech sounds, or they couldn't help him reach his goal. Later in the 1970s, as an undergraduate major in linguistics, he joined in the pursuit of learning to pronounce unusual sounds and transcribe unknown languages that was a major goal for students and teachers of languages at that time. Years later now, today's communicative teachers have been taught to focus primarily only on issues that impede communication, with the opinion that hyper-focusing on segmental issues would not improve overall communicative ability. Unfortunately, the proverbial baby was thrown out with the bathwater, and many teachers now enter the classroom unprepared to deal with pronunciation issues. Common exceptions to that trend can be found in those English language teachers who speak English as a second or foreign language (non-native English-speaking teachers, NNESTs), as they have more familiarity with explicitly describing the production of sounds, a skill that native English-speaking teachers (NESTs) will have acquired without instruction and without the ability to describe.

It was our goal to make our introductions of phonetics and phonology as approachable and accessible as possible, which is why the work strikes more of a conversational tone than a formal one. We try to present our information more as a discussion, which would be a continuation of the countless discussions the two of us have had with each other about these subjects.

We should also warn the reader that we have included what we hope is a great deal of humour in the text. Some may find the humour a bit disturbing and perhaps even inappropriate, but it is clear that when students are relaxed and enjoying what they read, they will learn more efficiently and retain more information. Both authors swore as students that their future books would never be as dull and boring as many of those they were forced to remain awake over were. Indeed, humour and especially the ability to make fun of oneself are keys to both teaching and learning better pronunciation habits. Remember that as we teach students a new language, they often think we are asking them to give up their precious identities. That is, of course, not our goal, but we can use humour to ease them into this brave new world of funny sounds and awkward movements.

As you begin reading this book, we think it would be helpful to share a couple of insights with you. First of all, as you can see, this book is very short. It is not meant to be a comprehensive guide to these topics, but instead is meant to serve as a brief introduction to the field. Much like the discussions we have had as a teacher and a student, it is meant to bridge the gap between linguistic theory and teacher training. The professional phonologist or phonetician may be dismayed at the cavalier attitude we have taken to some of the more controversial issues in the field. As our goal is to help the classroom teacher, not the budding phonetician, we have often not told the whole story. Doing so would trigger the law of diminishing returns and would overwhelm the reader with details that don't help teachers to be better pronunciation teachers. We do hope that if phonetics, phonology or pronunciation teaching enthralls you, you will go beyond this introductory text and explore the delightfully complex world of theory into which we barely peer. We would also like to draw your attention to the fact that both authors are American, and though we have tried our best to shed our dialectical default settings, we inevitably come back to examples that are rooted in our accent and/or dialect. We have been surprised, humbled and pleased that Palgrave/Macmillan Education, a publisher based in London, and both the senior commissioning editor and the series editor of the ALLC, who happen to speak British English, have chosen to accept two American authors for a work on pronunciation. Of course, you will notice that the editors have chosen to use standard British forms of orthography and punctuation rather than the original American versions we used as a matter of habit. That is fine with us because this is a book about pronunciation, not spelling. Indeed this cooperation is a testament to the truth that all language varieties are equal, even the offshoot dialect of a former recalcitrant colony. We do hope that you keep one point in mind as you incorporate what you learn about phonetics and phonology into your pronunciation teaching: it is not our place as teachers to elevate one dialect over another; rather, it is our job to help learners figure out what is most appropriate for their individual needs and their context. Enjoy the knowledge and the occasional bit of humour we hope you find here.

Series Editor's Introduction

The purpose of this Applied Linguistics for the Language Classroom (ALLC) series is to help bridge what still appears to be a significant gap between the field of applied linguistics and the day-to-day classroom realities of many language teachers and learners. For example, Selivan recently wrote that: "Much applied linguistics research remains unapplied, is often misapplied, or is downright inapplicable" (2016, p.25). This gap appears to have existed for some time, and has yet to be bridged. For example, in 1954, Pulgram published *Applied Linguistics In Language Teaching*, which was followed a few years later by Robert Lado's classic work, *Linguistics Across Cultures: Applied Linguistics for Language Teachers* (1957). However, we are still seeing articles 60 years later helping language teachers to apply linguistic theory to language lessons (Magrath, 2016).

Therefore, one of the features of this ALLC series that makes it distinctive is our focus on helping to bridge the ongoing gap between applied linguistics and language classrooms. Our envisaged readership for these books is busy classroom language teachers, including those entering the profession and those who have been in it for some time already. We also gave a lot of thought to what teachers completing a first degree in Education, teachers doing MA TESOL courses, and language teachers completing other professional qualifications, would find most useful and helpful.

Bearing such readers in mind, one of the ambitious goals of this ALLC series is to present language teachers with clear, concise and up-to-date overviews and summaries of what they need to know in key areas: Assessment; Methods and Methodologies; Technology; Research Methods; and Phonetics, Phonology and

Pronunciation. Attempting to do what much larger and weightier volumes have attempted, but doing so in volumes that are slimmer and more accessible, has been a challenge, but we believe these books make an original and creative contribution to the literature for language teachers.

Another distinctive feature of this ALLC series has been our International Advisory Board, made up of Professor Kathleen Bailey and Professor David Nunan. These two outstanding figures in our field helped us to keep our target readers in mind and to stay focused on the classroom, while keeping the connections to applied linguistics, so we can advance the building of the bridges between applied linguistics and language classrooms.

In *Phonetics, Phonology, & Pronunciation for the Language Classroom* Charles Hall and Christopher Hastings present a clear and concise introduction to and overview of three essential areas of language teaching and learning. Hall and Hastings take the readers on a journey, starting with a self-examination of the readers' beliefs about aspects of these three areas (Chapter 1) and ending with ten rules to guide the readers (Chapter 8). In between those two parts of the journey are hundreds of examples that helpfully illustrate the points they are making, from the Old Testament shibboleth to the tribes that still practise linguistic exogamy (see Chapter 4), resulting in every person in the village being multilingual from birth. There are also examples from many languages other than English, including Swedish, Danish and Norwegian, Arabic, German and Czech, Spanish, French, Dutch, and others.

Not only does the considerable combined teaching experience of more than 40 years of the two authors come across, from the first page to the last, but so too do their senses of humour. For example, when explaining the complex and potentially challenging concept of the *voiceless velar fricative* that appeared in words like *right, night, light,* and other 'silent' gh combinations, they write: "We assume that you never really thought (see what we did there?) about what the gh might (are you paying attention?) have been throughout (another one!) the history of English. Well, now you know, though (!), it might not be the most interesting thing you've ever learnt" (page 40).

Not only is their humour incorporated into giving examples, but also when giving advice. For example: "Please don't try to teach contrastive stress in isolation. It has to be in context. There are horrible exercises that ask students to change the stress in one sentence repeatedly. Don't do it!" (page 144). And in another example they write: "Not all scholars are convinced that teaching pronunciation only for communication and intelligibility will be sufficient to meet English language learners' needs. The simple answer is, of course, of course not!" (page 164). Such comments occur throughout the book, reflecting the fact that Hall and Hastings like to play with language, especially the sounds of English, but they are serious about helping teachers to develop their knowledge, skills and understanding of phonetics, phonology and pronunciation.

Hall and Hastings also make use of their own acronym PAY, which stands for Purpose, Audience and You. As they write in Chapter One: "We created PAY to serve as a mnemonic for teachers to use as an abbreviated needs analysis for each class. Using PAY, this book will help teachers realize that every learner has a different *purpose*, is part of a different *audience* and that *you* as the teacher have your own strengths and challenges" (page 9). As the PAY mnemonic shows, the focus is very much on teachers and learners, and giving practical advice.

As well as drawing on a large body of work, published from the early 1900s to 2016, the authors also draw extensively on their own experiences, personal as well as professional. For example, we learn that the first author is the godfather of a Czech child who was three years old when this book was being written, and that "both authors have seen spectacular lessons involving singing, chanting, and even dancing, but they both know that those are not methods that work for them" (page 118).

This book includes around 50 Activities designed to help the readers engage in hands-on exercises that will show how the theory works in practice, and how teachers can help their learners understand important fundamentals. In addition to the Activities, there are around 20 Suggested Readings, including material that is freely available online, with notes on each of the Readings, as well as a Glossary, giving brief definitions and descriptions of more than 100 technical terms from the fields of phonetics, phonology and pronunciation, which are emphasised throughout the text in bold.

Andy Curtis

Acknowledgements

Editors are often thanked pro forma, but in this case both the series editor Andy Curtis and Paul Stevens, Senior Commissioning Editor for Palgrave, do truly deserve thanks, awards, and medals for their endless patience and support, and for giving us the exact balance of encouragement and discouragement needed to help us reach our goal of a book that was valuable, novel and finished.

Charles feels compelled to thank his mother, father, sisters, nephews and godsons who unfailingly pay rapt attention to his harrowing stories about labialized consonants, dialect continua, and the Search for the Forbidden Sound. He also feels compelled to mention that they are all also accomplished actors.

Charles is extremely grateful to Dr Yasser Altamimi, the world's best boss, for perceptive and raucous conversations about phonology, teaching and Arabic coffee; John Fulghum for caustic criticism that actually helped; Dawn Arrol for brainstorming and brain-hurricanes about helping in-service teachers; Dan Harper for fiendishly brilliant ideas on how to incorporate pronunciation into TEFL training; Lorraine Meiners-Lovel for positive reactions to the strangest ideas about fingers and language; Anne Reef for helping him use language to see our world as wonderful, enthralling and truly mad; and Gabriela Klečková who is still helping him learn to pronounce [no^U]. And, of course, he wishes to thank his co-author Chris, the ring master of this circuitous circus, who made the project possible and who, in spite of Charles' starburst thoughts and so-called work habits, brought them through the storm with diplomacy and acumen.

Chris is grateful to the U.S. State Department English Language Programs and Georgetown University's Center for Intercultural Education and Development, which have allowed him the pleasure of working with thousands of teachers in China and Russia and gaining practical, classroom-based understanding of the topics central to this project. He is deeply indebted to the U.S. Department of State Regional English Language Officers, Kelli Odhuu and Jerrold Frank, both of whom offered him countless opportunities and support to grow as a teacher-trainer. Special thanks and gratitude are due to the staff and teachers of the Foreign Language Training Centre at ITMO University in St. Petersburg, Russia, who have helped him grow as a language teacher, a journey that is never finished. Finally, he would like to thank his wife, Josephine, and his four-year-old son, Stefan, who have provided excellent examples of L1-3 (Arabic, English and French) pronunciation issues while tolerating his absence from meals, bedtimes and vacations so that he might work on this book. And to them, both authors *dedicate* this book.

CHAPTER **1** **Introduction**

The purpose of this book is to give teachers access to practical aspects of phonetics, phonology and pronunciation. In this chapter, we lay out the road map for that journey, but let's first explore your own beliefs about language, accents, and learning and teaching pronunciation.

ACTIVITY 1.1

A. On paper, rate the following statements as *True*, *False*, *Maybe* or *Trick*, according to your beliefs. You will need your answers for the next activities.

1. Children get their accents from their parents.
2. Language X (your choice) is the hardest language to learn to speak.
3. You can't change the accent of someone who has been speaking English for a long time.
4. There are computer programs or language programs that can teach you to sound like a native.
5. We should try to help our students sound like native speakers so that they can blend in.
6. Everyone has an accent.
7. If I want to teach pronunciation, I have to learn anatomy and a new system of symbols.
8. We don't have enough class time to teach pronunciation.
9. Teaching pronunciation involves more than just individual sounds.

> 10. This book will give me all the techniques and tools I need to teach pronunciation.
> 11. There are some practical applications of phonetics and pronunciation.
>
> B. Compare your answers either with a partner or the class, according to the wishes of your instructor. Discuss why you chose what you did and see if your partners can change your mind or if you can change theirs.

Now let's look at the accepted 'truths' in our profession. How do these 'truths' compare with your intuitions or ideas? It may take a couple of classes to go over these eleven statements, so take your time. These answers might be called the 'accepted wisdom' of our profession. Notice that we didn't say 'the correct answer'. Having correct answers would be too easy. Rather, our 'model' answers reflect what we have learned from both experience and research so far. Perhaps there will be changes in what we believe in the future. Perhaps someone will develop a machine or pill that erases all traces of 'foreign' **accents**, although we doubt that will happen.

Remember that even if we say something is true or false, there will always be exceptions or rare cases, since we are dealing with humans. For example, even though Mozart composed music and played the violin and piano at the age of five, it is still a fact that children are not exceptional musicians at five.

1. Children get their accents from their parents. *False.* This fact bothers parents, but children *acquire* (unconsciously learn) their accents from their peers and the children who are just a little older than they are. And no, it's not teachers who teach children to speak their native language either. If it were the case that children acquired their accents from their parents, the children of immigrants would have 'foreign' accents. In spite of their father's famous accent, Arnold Schwarzenegger's children speak with a standard American English accent, as they grew up in California.

Even more convincing is the fact that the **hearing children** *of deaf parents* **speak** the language of their hearing peers absolutely normally, or that the ***deaf children*** *of hearing parents* are able to **sign** without a non-native 'accent' in their signed language.

2. Language X is the hardest language to learn to speak. *Maybe.* Let's quickly get the idea that everyone learns languages at the same speed, the same way or even for the same reason out of the picture immediately. Each learner and indeed each learning context is unique. How difficult a language is for each learner depends on many factors that we explore later in Chapters 4 and 7.

Let's briefly say that the ease or difficulty of learning a language generally depends on the age at which learners started to learn to speak that new language and what language(s) they spoke before. It may even depend on the type of society they come from. And perhaps most importantly, it depends on the motivation of the learner. So, yes, this is a very definite 'maybe'.

If you think English, or any other language for that matter, is the hardest language to learn, you are both right and wrong. It depends on who is doing the learning. Regardless of the relative difficulty in learning English, as you will see in Chapter 6, English has become the world's first truly international or global language, so we can refer to **English as an International Language** (EIL). We can even refer to it as **English as a Lingua Franca** (ELF), a term we explore in Chapter 6.

The global status of English means that it must be learnable, but learning to speak can mean many things. For some learners, it might mean trying to sound as if they grew up in Dallas, London or Toronto. For others, it might be fine just to be fluent enough in English to be able to communicate a simple request for a cup of coffee with someone from a different country who doesn't share their first language.

3. You can't change the accent of someone who's been speaking English for a while. *Maybe.* For many years, the term **fossilized** was used to say that once a learner's accent was, well, fossilized, it couldn't be altered. As we will see in Chapter 4, there is evidence that targeted **pronunciation** instruction can change accents for some speakers. However, again the word *motivation* is the main issue. Why would a speaker want to spend the effort to modify his or her accent if that person has been successful in communicating for years already? There must be a highly motivating reason or two to make the effort necessary to change worthwhile.

4. There are computer programs or language programs that can teach you to sound like a native. *False.* Well, it is false now, and it is likely to remain false for some time. It is true that some computer programs can help you a bit, but if a program were enough, the major computer-based language programs wouldn't be offering you a chance to interact with live human tutors for an additional fee.

One of the real problems in using computer programs, or even instructors for that matter, for pronunciation issues is that as an adult, you can't even hear the differences in sounds that might be important in a specific language. In Chapter 3, you will learn about **phonemes**, the significant sounds of a language. Sadly, usually once a person is in her or his late teens, the ability to distinguish all possible human language sounds is turned off. You basically only 'hear' (in other words, are able to notice) the differences that are important for your language(s). For example, you most likely know that it is usually difficult for speakers of English and most languages related to English (called the *Indo-European languages*) to distinguish between the **tones** of Chinese and the many other languages with developed tone systems because we don't have tones at the word level. Most likely you can't consistently hear the difference in the sound file in the four different words in Chinese that are all 'spelled' *ma – mā, má, mǎ* and *mà* – that mean 'mother', 'bother', 'horse' and 'scold', respectively. The different tones are significant for Chinese speakers, but not for speakers of many other languages. That is an example of the 'negative' influence of the native language in learning a foreign language. The computer can't hear those differences for you and can't really teach you to make the difference any better than an instructor could and usually not as well. That said, there are some advances in feedback that may (and let's stress *may*) be very effective in the future. Nonetheless, in Chapter 7, we discuss some uses of technology that can help, but they aren't perfect. However, our motto is whatever works.

5. We should try to help our students sound like native speakers so that they can blend in. *False.* Unless you work for the CIA, SIS, MSS, GRU or another spy agency, or some call centres (and even they aren't that successful), your goal should be intelligibility, not native speaker accuracy. Sounding like a native speaker would need to be the student's goal (not the teacher's goal for the student), and even then most learners aren't successful.

It also is practical and realistic to say that our goal is **intelligibility**, as it is almost impossible to make adults, or even those in their late teens, sound 'native'. As a side note, there is a lively discussion about whether 'native' accents actually do exist and what can be considered one; we discuss this further in Chapter 6. People who have learned a new language as adults and who manage to 'pass' as native speakers in a second language are the exceptions to the rule, for sure. Let's return to Arnold Schwarzenegger. In spite of his obvious Austrian accent, he was elected governor of California. His accent didn't hinder him; his 'strong' (a value judgement word we would prefer not to use) accent might have even helped, since it gave him a strong identity. If he had sounded just like any other American politician, he might not have been as successful. Of course, groups always consider some accents good and others bad. Educated Americans often swoon over an upper-class British accent or any French accent while often viewing other accents as déclassé(s) or ugly, but that is a subjective opinion and not an objective fact. In theory, all accents, dialects and languages are equal. But just as was said in George Orwell's *Animal Farm*, some 'are more equal than others'.

On the other hand, you might think about the seemingly endless list of Australian and British actors, such as Cate Blanchett, Hugh Laurie, Nicole Kidman or Simon Baker, who sound completely American in films and on television. Remember, however, that you only hear the success stories. If a mistake in accent/pronunciation is made during filming, the director shouts, 'Cut', and the mistake is erased. People don't get that chance when speaking in real-life situations. Also, these actors are exceptions, not the norm. Just think of how many truly dreadful fake British, Spanish and French accents in English you've heard from many Americans or British people. We'll talk more about the distinction between *intelligibility* and *accent* later on in Chapter 4.

6. Everyone has an accent. *True.* Yes, everyone has an accent. Many British and Americans think that their English is accent-free. First, both groups can't be right. If they didn't have an American/British accent, how would we know that they speak 'perfect' British or American? It is human nature to think that other people have accents; sadly, it's an 'us versus them' world. In Chapters 2 and 3, we discuss sounds and accents and see how even 'standard' accents can change over time. For example, not many Americans now pronounce the words *caught/cot* differently although there 'should' theoretically be a difference in Standard American English (SAE). However, that difference is disappearing in the United States. We call a pair of words, such as *caught/cot* that have, or should have, one difference in sound (not spelling!) a **minimal pair**. Other examples of minimal pairs would be *park/bark*, *rat/sat* or even *wind* (it up) and a (strong) *wind*, as we are listening to sounds, not looking at spelling.

ACTIVITY 1.2

True or false? Are the following pairs of words minimal pairs – that is do the words differ in exactly one sound? Say the words aloud to make sure you aren't being misled by spelling.

1. _____ polish (shoes)/Polish (person)
2. _____ great/grate
3. _____ sing/sung
4. _____ boy/toy
5. _____ though/dough

The accent issue also brings us back to intelligibility. Can the listener understand the speaker? Notice that we define intelligibility in terms of the listener, not the speaker. In Chapter 4, we look at research that shows that accent and intelligibility aren't always so easily related. A speaker can have a 'strong foreign accent' (there is that value judgement again) and still be very intelligible.

7. If I want to teach pronunciation, I have to learn anatomy and a new system of symbols. *Trick.* It helps to learn a few new parts of the mouth, such as the *velum* (soft **palate**) or the *uvula* (that thing that dangles at the back of your throat) or the *alveolar* (gum) ridge, as you will in Chapter 2. Generally, however, you will use basic terms you already know. Likewise, it helps to know the most common symbols of the **International Phonetic Alphabet** (IPA) to discuss pronunciation; however, you know most of the symbols for the most part from just knowing how to read the Latin alphabet (that's the one used in English). It's more an effort not to confuse letters with sounds. For example, the IPA symbol [g], shown in square brackets, always represents the first sound in *ghost*, never the first sound in *giraffe*; the first sound in *giraffe* is represented with [dž] by most Europeans and by [ǰ] by many Americans. After you go through Chapter 2, you will be able to transcribe most English words with a degree of accuracy. Knowing those symbols will help you be precise when teaching pronunciation, but it's not at all difficult. It is more important that you be able to 'read' the symbols than be able to produce them.

8. We don't have enough time to teach pronunciation. *False.* After WWII, there was a method you will learn more about in Chapter 4 that emphasized extensive repetition of sounds and oral dialogues, called the **Audio-lingual Method** (ALM). Students would spend hours in the language lab repeating minimal pairs, pairs of words that differ by exactly one sound, such as *sheep/ship*, into a tape recorder. For a very few students, that was effective; for most, it was a waste of time, tape and tempers. That experience left us with a bad taste in our mouth about pronunciation teaching.

Today, however, we know that targeted, extremely quick, explicit instruction (which the first author of this book calls **lightning drills**) can be very effective. We have learned that this truly is a case of 'less is more'. Think of these drills as a special case of '**comprehensible input**' that you create by focusing entirely on one form for a very brief period. By using lightning drills when appropriate, we can help our students improve through focused, appropriate intervention. If your students have no problem at all consistently saying the first sound represented by *th* in *thanks, thin, thick* or *thread* correctly, there is no reason to spend even a minute practising that sound just because there is an exercise in the textbook about it. We have plenty of time for the right kind of pronunciation teaching when it is necessary. Of course, that means that your first job is to determine what your students need to improve; every class will be slightly different, even if students are all from the same background. Finding out what your students need (and sometimes want) is called a needs analysis, which should be part of every teacher's basic activities. We use the mnemonic **PAY** (purpose, audience, you) to help remember to carry out an extremely simplistic form of needs analysis everytime you enter a classroom.

9. Teaching pronunciation involves more than just individual sounds. *True.* As we see in Chapter 5, aspects of language, such as **stress, prosody** and **intonation**, which we call **suprasegmentals**, are also crucial in teaching language. Think of the early computer-generated voices. Each word existed in a universe of its own and sounded very odd. Today, some computers have been programmed with intonation, and sound much more natural. The same is true for language learners. At the same time, we will destroy the belief that teaching these aspects is difficult.

10. This book will give me all the techniques and tools I need to teach pronunciation. *Trick.* Obviously, a short book this size cannot begin to cover everything a teacher could or should know about pronunciation teaching. Instead, this book gives teachers a good start they can use as they learn to evaluate the PAY (purpose, audience and you) of each different learner and class. We created PAY to serve as a mnemonic for teachers to use as an abbreviated needs analysis for each class. Using PAY, this book helps teachers realize that every learner has a different *purpose*, is part of a different *audience* and that *you* as the teacher have your own strengths and challenges. Together these factors create PAY that permeates our discussion of teaching pronunciation. In fact, it forms the fourth *P* that we could add to the three *P*s in the title of this book. If you are teaching now, stop and think about the PAY(s) of your class(es). If you are not teaching, think about possible PAYs. If you have been a language learner, do you think your instructors ever thought about the PAY? Or did they think they were just teaching non-existent so-called 'General English'? In fact, the ESP (English for Specific Purposes) expert Professor Liz England always jokes about TENAR – Teaching English for No Apparent Reason. This text helps you discover the PAYs you need and helps you teach for very apparent reasons.

ACTIVITY 1.3

We ask you to write a descriptive paragraph about yourself in the next activity, but for now, choose where you think you fit along these continua that describe different traits that influence how/what/why you teach. Remember that none of these traits is 'right' or 'wrong'. Rate how you are, not how you wish you could be or think you should be because someone once erroneously told you that 'all good teachers are...'. You may also be surprised by some of our dichotomies, but they've been chosen to assess what kind of a pronunciation teacher you might be or become. Were we talking about writing or grammar, they might be different.

1. _____ loud ...1...2...3...4...5... quiet
2. _____ likes deviating from plans ...1...2...3...4...5... hates deviating from plans
3. _____ organized ...1...2...3...4...5... disorganized
4. _____ wants theory ...1...2...3...4...5... wants results
5. _____ introvert ...1...2...3...4...5... extrovert
6. _____ native speaker of English ...1...2...3...4...5... non-native
7. _____ lesson plans ...1...2...3...4...5... teachable moments
8. _____ likes people ...1...2...3...4...5... likes books
9. _____ expert user of English ...1...2...3...4...5... non-expert
10. _____ male ...1...2...3...4...5... female

Compare your results with those of classmates, and predict how each of these pairs might influence what kind of a teacher each pair represents. What traits do you think would also be important for teaching pronunciation? Are there any traits that would be important for all types of teaching?

ACTIVITY 1.4

Write a descriptive paragraph about yourself and the type of teacher you are or think you will be. Although we can all improve, there is no right answer.

11. There are some practical applications of phonetics and pronunciation. *True.* We would imagine that you thought that statement was either false or a trick. For example, the use of pronunciation to separate friend from foe in warfare is as old as humankind, it appears. In the *Book of Judges*, a book of the (Old Testament/Hebrew) Bible, there is the story of the **shibboleth**, which originally just meant a stalk of grain. Once two closely related groups were fighting each other. As they didn't wear uniforms and were closely related, it was difficult to tell friend from foe. When suspected members of the losing group (the foe) were caught trying to sneak back to their own land, they were ordered to say that word: *shibboleth*. Unfortunately, for them, there was no *sh* [š] sound in their dialect. As a result, they said *sibboleth* [sic] instead, as this was the way the word was pronounced in their dialect. Upon hearing the 'wrong' pronunciation, the winners killed those speakers. Since then, the word *shibboleth* has come to mean anything (a custom, a word, clothing, etc.) that separates one group from another, often in a negative sense. There are many other examples of pronunciation shibboleths throughout history that were used to separate friend from foe, usually resulting in a quick death for the speaker on the 'wrong' side of the pronunciation divide, such as the somewhat apocryphal Parsley Massacre in the Dominican Republic in 1937. It is said that Dominican soldiers distinguished between Dominican and Haitian civilians by asking them to pronounce the word *perejil* (parsley) and let them live or killed them on the basis of their pronunciation.

Pronunciation is indeed a major marker of group identity. A modern shibboleth is the pronunciation of the diphthong (type of **vowel** sound) in words such as *about* or *house* in many parts of Canada. Some American comedians love to make fun of the Canadian pronunciation of the sound represented most often by *ou* because it serves as a clear marker of people from that country. Not all Canadians use that pronunciation (yet?), but enough that it's become a shibboleth.

Fortunately, most of us will never have to use **phonetics** and pronunciation to identify terrorists, as is sometimes done today, or to kill our enemies, but we do use pronunciation every day to decide if people are 'like us or not like us'. As the Irish playwright George Bernard Shaw (1913) wrote: 'It is impossible for an Englishman to open his mouth without making some other Englishman hate or despise him.' In that way, learning to talk about pronunciation can be very practical for us as teachers who are trying to help learners of English find their way in our societies and our world.

These eleven statements have helped us explore some of the more controversial issues of phonetics, **phonology** and pronunciation. Let's now go to a quick overview of each of the chapters so that you will know what to expect.

Overview of the Chapters

Chapter 2: Phonetics: Sounds and Symbols: We learn how human language sounds are produced and heard. Concentrating mainly on how sounds are produced, articulatory phonetics, you learn to transcribe and interpret the major notational systems, mainly the International Phonetic Alphabet (IPA), used for phonetics in ELT.

Chapter 3: Phonology: Language Systems: After examining the isolated sounds of language, we consider how sounds are combined to create phonological systems. More importantly, we explore how phonological systems from learners' native languages influence Second Language Acquisition (SLA) in speech, writing and even reading. Using contrastive analysis, teachers learn to use their new knowledge to address issues arising from language or dialect differences they may encounter in their classrooms or work.

Chapter 4: Research and Pronunciation: After examining human sounds and sound systems, we look at the role of teaching pronunciation in major methodologies and approaches of English Language Teaching (ELT). We then survey scholarly and classroom research into producing and receiving spoken language, and identify gaps in the literature. The chapter ends with an extensive look at how best to identify and implement strategies for integrating pronunciation instruction in both the heterogeneous and homogenous classroom.

Chapter 5: Suprasegmentals: Bigger Than Words: This chapter examines the features of speech that include *tone, stress, prosody* and *intonation*. After examining the major views on the role of these and other suprasegmentals in language teaching, we ask readers to determine appropriate goals and techniques for identifying prosodic features of speech as well as rules and practice exercises to make the appropriate teaching of suprasegmentals more effective.

Chapter 6: Language Varieties and English as a Lingua Franca: The emergence of English as a Lingua Franca (ELF) has led to a shared ownership of the varieties of English by both native speakers (NS) and non-native speakers (NNS). This chapter discusses the topic of ELF as it relates to the teaching and learning of pronunciation in ESL and EFL contexts. It then develops the conversation further to examine the role of language varieties in the teaching of second and foreign languages. We refer to recent work that has been done on accent and identity, while asking readers to determine their own stance on the issues. Special emphasis is given to the role of non-native teachers in the teaching of pronunciation as the majority of English teachers throughout the world are in fact non-natives.

Chapter 7: Technology and Pronunciation Teaching: This chapter first examines the history of the use and misuse of technology in teaching pronunciation and asks teachers to determine how they best think technology can be used to help students. Then, readers are shown how new research or technologies can provide better understanding of how to teach pronunciation and how teachers themselves can become better researchers. Finally, we ask teachers to reflect on how new technologies can be used appropriately to help students both understand and produce language.

Chapter 8: Final Thoughts: In this final chapter, we ask teachers to consider how they will continue to be both teachers and researchers in pronunciation. At the same time, we ask them to develop their own approach to implementing (or not implementing) pronunciation instruction into different curricula and syllabi.

Before we turn to the basic elements of language, individual sounds and phonetics, let's see if you have changed your mind about any of the eleven statements.

ACTIVITY 1.5

Quickly go over what you wrote about the eleven statements again, and see if you have changed your mind about any of your answers. As you worked through the statements of 'accepted wisdom', what surprised you most? Which are you still not sure about? What would it take to convince you?

Suggested Readings

Darcy, I., D. Ewert and R. Lidster (2012) Bringing Pronunciation Instruction Back into the Classroom: An ESL Teachers' Pronunciation 'Toolbox', in J. Levis and K. LeVelle, *Proceedings of the 3rd Annual Pronunciation in Second Language Learning and Teaching Conference* (Ames, IA: Iowa State University), pp. 93–108 (accessed from http://jlevis.public.iastate.edu/Proceedingsfrom3rdPSLLT%20updated.pdf#page=98).

This short article provides the reader with a quick and accurate overview of the problems faced by those who wish to teach pronunciation. More importantly, it provides a case study of how pronunciation can be implemented in an Intensive English Programme (IEP). The authors present good ideas on what the focus of pronunciation should be as English ability grows. This article appears in the third annual proceedings of one of the few annual conferences devoted to the teaching of pronunciation.

Grant, L. J., with D. Brinton and T. Derwing, M. J. Munro, J. Field, J. Gilbert, J. Murphy, et al. (2014) *Pronunciation Myths: Applying Second Language Research to Classroom Teaching* (Ann Arbor: University of Michigan Press).

Linda Grant is one of the most important voices in contemporary pronunciation instruction, especially in North America. In this volume, she has gathered many of the other major researchers in pronunciation. The prologue, written by Professor Grant, is an excellent overview of what areas teachers should know; although she says it is addressed to 'informed practitioners', you should work your way through the prologue slowly, noting what seems completely unknown and what you already know. After you finish our book, you should reread this prologue to see if you agree with her, and indeed with us, on what is important.

CHAPTER 2 Phonetics

> This chapter introduces the study of phonetics by helping readers become aware of the entire range of human language sounds and how they are produced and received. By leading language teachers through the basics of both articulatory and acoustic phonetics, they will understand the mechanics of sound production and sound perception. At the same time, they will learn to transcribe and interpret the major notational systems used for phonetics in ELT, such as the International Phonetic Alphabet (IPA).

Although language is possible without sounds, as writing and sign language demonstrate, spoken language is remarkable because a limited number of sounds can be combined to create an unlimited number of words, sentences, texts and ideas. To explore these sounds of human language, we follow the traditional division between vowels (sounds that can 'stand alone') and **consonants**.

You will have to learn a few new symbols, but your hardest task will be unlearning years of **hyperliteracy** that causes you to think of the written text as primary and the spoken as its derivative. *Hyperliteracy* is an invented word we use to emphasize that educated English users usually view the written word, rather than the spoken form, as the norming form. Hyperliteracy has led to many 'spelling pronunciations' for words such as *palm* (of your hand) in which the *l* wasn't originally pronounced and served as a written symbol with no overt phonetic value to distinguish the pronunciation of *Pam* from *palm*. You might know other words whose pronunciation has changed because people looked at the spelling instead of listening, such as *Anthony, almond* or *forehead.* To teach pronunciation effectively, you need to divorce sound from English *orthography* (spelling) and truly listen to sounds, not read them.

ACTIVITY 2.1

Let's explore some of the ways English orthography complicates the teaching of pronunciation.
1. _____ Which letter is not pronounced? limb, comb, bomb, lamb, debt
2. _____ Which word rhymes with *great*? meat, meet, mate
3. _____ Which vowel *sound* is not like the others? though, through, dough, slow
4. _____ Which *th* sound is different from the other three? thin, thread, the, theatre
5. _____ How do the two *convicts* differ? 'Convict the convict!' said the victim.

Language Sounds

We rarely think about the sounds of language. Perhaps we might remark that someone has an unfamiliar accent. Normally, however, unless something goes awry (such as trying to learn a foreign language), we rarely give the sounds of our native languages a thought. Even when we are frustrated at our inability to understand a non-native speaker of our own language, we almost never think in terms of the individual sounds. When we do consider individual sounds, we have entered the realm of phonetics.

For now, a loose analysis of the word *phonetics* is sufficient. The final *–s* is familiar from other sciences, such as mathematics, physics or logistics. That suffix is just a nominalizer; it makes the stem a noun. We recognize that the **phon-** means 'sound', as in *telephone* (far sound) or *phonograph* (written sound). That leaves only the *-etic* suffix. We discuss this in more explicit terms in the next chapter, but for now we can define it as 'all possible differences humans are capable of detecting'. As a result, phonetics is the science of looking at all the different (human speech) sounds that vary in some way. It is important to note that no adult is capable of hearing or producing the differences in all possible human sounds. In *Pygmalion*, the play that was adapted into the musical *My Fair Lady*, a phonetician confesses that he is only able to produce 24 vowel sounds, whereas the protagonist, Henry Higgins, can produce 130 (Shaw, 1913).

The reverse is also true; unless there are physical or other handicaps, hearing infants are capable of distinguishing all possible human language sounds at birth. Obviously, they can't produce them automatically; they must practise using muscles to speak just as they must practise using their muscles to walk. Unfortunately for those who wish to learn a new language, we all lose that innate ability as we age (and for this process, fourteen years of age is already 'old'), and eventually we only concentrate on those sounds that are important in our particular linguistic environment.

Because we are genetically programmed to unconsciously acquire and adapt to the sounds of our native or childhood languages, we can be frustrated as adults when we study phonetics, the possible sounds of human languages, and find that we have lost that inborn ability to perceive and eventually produce all possible human sounds. Remember we are discussing prototypical children. Obviously, some children have trouble pronouncing *s* sounds in English and lisp, and others cannot produce the English *r*. But in general, all human children can produce and perceive all possible human sounds and differences. The first time we might consider individual sounds might be when we attempt to consciously *learn* (as opposed to the unconscious *acquiring* that children do) a new language. For example, we might comment that the French or Spanish *r* sound is difficult. We may notice that many Spanish speakers seem to be unable to hear or produce the difference in the initial sounds of the words *boat* and *vote*. Then we go on about our day. The overt investigation of phonetics is rarely important to the average adult. That changes when we attempt to learn or teach a second language.

For over a century, there have been two primary threads of study in phonetics. First, there is **articulatory phonetics**, which describes how sounds are made; then there is *acoustic phonetics*, which describes how we hear sounds. A more recent addition to the mix is auditory phonetics, which focuses on the hearing and perception of speech sounds. In this chapter, we focus almost exclusively on articulatory phonetics.

To begin, we need to look at the general anatomy of the speech process. Humans are a bit like bagpipes. We use our lungs to inhale air to replenish oxygen, and to exhale air to rid the body of carbon dioxide. Sometime a couple of hundred million years ago along the evolutionary path, vertebrates tacked another purpose on the lungs that had developed from the fish ancestors' digestive tracts: pushing air through the vocal tract to make sounds. Again almost a couple of hundred of million years later, humans put that ability to use to create language. Now, by pulling air in and pushing it out through the vocal tract, we can discuss language.

Most of the sounds of language are made by exhaling air. Put your finger directly on your lips, and try to lengthen the first sound in the name *Hall*. You can feel the air rushing out of mouth. That is an *explosive* sound.

Only a few language sounds are made by inhaling air. For example, in some forms of Swedish, you can signal agreement by inhaling a word similar to *you*. While inhaling, say *you*. Those sounds are rare. Vietnamese has *implosive* sounds that give the language a 'popping' character to speakers of other languages. Implosive sounds are rare and not essential in English, so we won't discuss them further.

Let's continue our tour of the vocal tract and explore the sounds of English. There are many humanly possible sounds that English doesn't use, and we only touch on a few of those sounds to illustrate some basic principles. First, however, we need a writing system that will help us create a one-to-one relationship between a symbol and a sound.

Standard English orthography is notoriously fickle (consider the many pronunciations of *–ough* in *cough, through, thorough* or *thought*), so we use a slightly modified version of the IPA that was developed by linguists at the end of the nineteenth century. The IPA was created so that everyone writing or reading about language sounds could be confident about the sound of the symbol or letter being used. For example, in the IPA, an [f] always represents the last sound in *off* and never the last sound in *of* (that is a [v] sound). To show that we are using the IPA and not English, French, German or Vietnamese spelling, we put square brackets around IPA symbols: [f]. Square brackets indicate the actual sound that comes out of the mouth. In the next chapter, we learn how to show 'mental' sounds. Fortunately, you already know most of the symbols we use here. Your task is to remember that each symbol always has the same sound; for example, [g] is always the sound in *ago* and never the sound in *gem*.

ACTIVITY 2.2

Many of the IPA symbols represent the same basic sound as the corresponding English letter. Your task is to distinguish between sound and orthography.

1. _____ [g] = the sound in *go*. Which *g* is not [g]? ghost, ghoul, tough, ago
2. _____ [k] = the sound in *kite*. Which word has a [k]? chaos, church, chin, chic
3. _____ [s] = the sound in *so*. Which *s* is not [s]? sin, his, cats, missing
4. _____ [d] = the sound in *do*. Which *d* is not [d]? did, asked, buzzed, bud
5. _____ [f] = the sound in *f*. Which *f* is not [f]? off, fine, effort, of

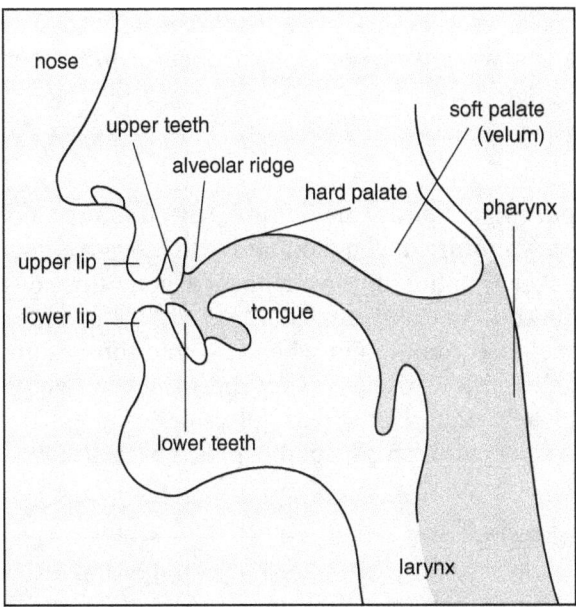

Figure 2.1 Cross-section of head

For English, and most languages, we need to discuss sounds along three parameters: where the sound is made (*place of articulation*), how the sound is made (*manner of articulation*) and voicing, which we define later. Let's begin with a tour of the major areas in the mouth and throat that are essential in pronouncing English. Figure 2.1 should help you visualize a cross-section of the mouth to identify the major places sounds are articulated.

Labials

We begin our tour at the entrance to the mouth, with the lips. In science, *bi-* means 'two', as in *bipolar* or *bicycle*. Likewise, most know that **labial** means 'lips'. Combining those two parts, we can say that sounds made with the two lips are *bilabial*. That term, *bilabial*, describes the *place of articulation*. Next, we need to describe how we make a sound, the *manner of articulation*.

Stops

Place your finger lightly on your lips; say *oh* for as long as you can. Once you started, you didn't have to move your lips. Now, try *Oh, Papa!* Notice that you opened your lips to say the vowels but had to close your mouth to say the two [p] sounds. The air stopped coming out when you said those sounds. You stopped the airflow for just a very short time, but you stopped it completely. Sounds such as [p] – notice the IPA square brackets – are called **stops**. So, the [p] is a *bilabial stop*.

Minimal Pairs

Now say *Oh, baby!* The airflow stops when you say [b], which is also a bilabial stop. You know there is a difference between [b] and [p]. How? As a proficient English speaker, you recognize that there are *minimal pairs* that differ only in one sound but clearly mean different things. For example, *bark* and *park* form a minimal pair that proves that the difference we hear between [p] and [b] is significant in English. That means there must be some yet undiscussed factor that distinguishes the two sounds. It's called *voicing*.

Voicing

Let's describe this noticeable difference with a pair of sounds. Grasp the front of your own neck with your flattened hand as if you were choking yourself. Say the sound [z] as in *Zane* for as long as you can. You feel strong vibration in your throat. You can also hear that vibration with your fingers in your ears or with your hand on top of your head. Try all three methods in the privacy of your home or in a phonetics class. That is voicing, the vibration of the vocal cords in your *larynx* (Adam's apple). In other words, this [z] as in *Zane* is a **voiced** sound.

Now say the [s] as in *sane*. You feel no vibration. Your vocal cords are not vibrating, so the [s] is a **voiceless** sound. Alternate between the sounds with one hand around your throat: [s], [z], [s], [z], [s], [z], [s] and [z]. You automatically turn the voicing on and off as you make those sounds. The minimal pair *sane* and *Zane* demonstrates that voicing is significant in English.

Returning to the bilabial stop pair *bark* and *park*, we see that it is voicing that distinguishes the bilabial stops from each other. Put one hand around your throat and whisper *a park* and then *a bark*. You should be able to feel the vibration in <u>b</u>ark, but none in <u>p</u>ark. That means that [b] is a *voiced bilabial stop*, whereas [p] is a *voiceless bilabial stop* in English.

ACTIVITY 2.3

Voicing can be a little difficult to feel or hear at first. Relax and take your time.

A. Working in pairs, determine which of these words ends in a voiced consonant. Compare your results with those of the class.

1. _____ mass/maze
2. _____ raid/rate
3. _____ lug/luck
4. _____ rip/rib
5. _____ breath/breathe

B. Working in pairs, determine which of these words begins with a voiceless consonant. Compare your results with those of the class.

6. _____ pair/bear
7. _____ vase/face
8. _____ chin/gin
9. _____ zoo/sue
10. _____ den/ten

Nasals

We have another sound with a different *manner of articulation* in English that is also bilabial. Say *mama mia*. Instead of putting your finger on your lips, give yourself a moustache by putting one finger right under your nose. As you say [m], your lips will remain closed, but you will feel a tiny bit of air coming out of your nose. We stop the airflow from coming out of our mouth but switch it over to come out of our nose. You know the adjectival form of the word for *nose* is *nasal*, so [m] is a bilabial **nasal**. Don't worry about voicing for nasals.

We now know that we have three bilabial sounds in English. Other languages, such as Japanese and Spanish, have other bilabial sounds, but we'll ignore those since we are only talking about English. Table 2.1 shows what we have so far learned about bilabial sounds:

Table 2.1   English bilabial consonants

Place of Articulation	Manner of Articulation		
	Stop		Nasal
	Voiceless	Voiceless	
Bilabial	[p]	[b]	[m]

We will continue to add to this chart until we have all the places and manners of articulation we need for Standard American English.

Labiodentals

Let's move further into the mouth just a bit. Gently bite your lower lip with your upper teeth. Using scientific terms, we would call that place of articulation **labiodental** (*labio* = 'lip' and *dental* = 'teeth'). We're not aware of any languages that make a sound by touching the bottom teeth to the upper lip, so we don't need two terms.

Friction: Fricatives

Say *fire*. Notice that you are pushing air through the tiny gap that is formed when we barely touch our lower lips with our upper teeth. That first sound in *fire* is the *labiodental* sound [f]. Is it a stop or a nasal? Neither. Everyone has small gaps in and around the teeth, so it would be almost impossible to completely stop the airflow that way. That sound is similar to a nasal in that you can continue to say [f] or [m] until you run out of air. Vowels are similar in the same way. So what separates the [f] from an [m], as in *me* or the vowel sound in *fee*?

Let's return to the [s] and [z] sounds. Contrast the [s] sound in *see* and the *vowel* in *foe*. For the [s], your mouth is almost closed and there is a great deal of audible friction like the hissing of a snake. On the other hand, for the vowel sound in *foe*, your mouth is open and there is no friction. As a result, we call sounds such as [s], [z] and [f] **fricatives** because they produce friction and can be held for as long as you have air. So, [f] is a *labiodental fricative*.

Voiced/Voiceless Pairs

One of the characteristics of Modern English is that most of the consonants come in voiced/voiceless pairs. We've already seen the pairs [z]/[s] and [b]/[p]. We should expect there to be a 'twin' for the [f] sound as well. Using your voicing test, you can determine that [f] is voiceless. That means that we need a voiced partner for it. Say this pair and see if you think it's a minimal pair: *fine/vine*. Both initial sounds, [f] and [v], are labiodental fricatives, so we have another voiced/voiceless pair: [v]/[f].

This is a good point to remind readers that the IPA symbols refer only to sounds, not letters. Take the word *of*. It ends in the letter *f*, but the final sound is [v]. You need to be careful not to confuse spelling with transcribing, the technical term for writing down sounds in the IPA. Now look at the German car name *Volkswagen*. If you said it 'correctly' the letter *v* is pronounced [f] while the *w* is pronounced [v]. The spelling of *Volkswagen* reflects German orthography, but we still use the same IPA symbols no matter how the sound is spelled.

Between the Teeth: Interdentals

We've already discussed why we can't have labiodental stops or labiodental nasals, so we continue on to the most difficult pair of sounds for most learners of English. Say *thigh*. Either look in a mirror or at a partner as he or she says it. For most English speakers, you can see that the tip of the tongue actually sticks out from between the teeth a bit as you say it. Exaggerate the initial *th* sound and you will clearly see your tongue. To produce that *th* sound, you stick your tongue between your teeth and push air out in an unbroken stream. Translating that description into scientific terms, we can say that it is an **interdental** sound. We also know that we can hold that sound as long as we want and that it produces a bit of friction, so it must be an interdental fricative. Stop for a moment and now consider how difficult this sound must be for learners of English in terms of politeness. Yes, we have to ask our students to 'stick their tongues out' at people. If you are a native speaker of English or Icelandic, and certain forms of Spanish or Arabic, you don't notice the 'rude' action required to pronounce those sounds because it's just your language, but if the learner of any of those languages doesn't already have interdental sounds, it's really difficult to break years of social conditioning. Thinking back to PAY (purpose/audience/you), you can see that whether these sounds will be problematic will be determined by the audience and perhaps even by you if you happen not to use the interdental sounds in your variety (native or learned) of English. Now back to the simple problems of phonetics.

We have a problem. A basic rule of the IPA is that one symbol represents one sound, and one sound is represented by one symbol. For historical reasons, English has developed a couple of two-letter combinations that together represent one sound. The *th* is one example, and the other major examples are *ph* as in *phone* or *sh* as in *shoe*. There are actually other ways to write the same sound as *sh* (as in techni*ci*an) or *ph* (as in *fi*sh). Indeed, as has been pointed out, there is a bit of irony in the fact that *phonetic* is spelled with *ph*- instead of *f*-. On the other hand, there is no other way to represent the *th* sounds in English.

Because we use two letters to represent one sound, we call those letter combinations **digraphs** (literally 'two letters'). We cannot use a digraph in the IPA, so a new symbol had to be used. Actually, an old symbol had to be recycled. If you learned the Greek letters because you belonged to an American sorority or fraternity (which use Greek letters as their names), you might know that the Greek letter θ is called *theta* and has the *th* sound as its initial sound. We would begin the transcription of *thigh* as [θ...].

We've solved the one symbol/one sound problem, but we must figure out if θ, an interdental fricative, is voiced or voiceless. In the time-honoured manner, put your hand tightly around your neck and say *thin*. Was it voiced or voiceless? Let's hope you said voiceless. That means that θ is a *voiceless interdental fricative*. You also should remember that almost all English consonants come in voiceless/voiced pairs, and θ is no exception.

Here we run into another problem with regular English *orthography* – spelling. There are really two *th* sounds, and they are both represented by the digraph *th*- in English writing. As native speakers, we automatically and unconsciously hear the difference between the voiced and voiceless forms, so it isn't that confusing for us in daily life. By now, you should know that we will look for a minimal pair to prove they are different. If you say *either* with the same vowel as in *fee*, then *either/ether* is a minimal pair. Just in case you aren't familiar with the second word, *ether* is an early type of anaesthetic. This isn't a minimal pair for those who say *either* with the same vowel as in *five*. For those speakers for whom *either/ether* isn't a minimal pair, we can use the slightly salacious minimal pair *thy/thigh*. Which is voiceless and which is voiced? How do we represent the voiced partner of the [θ]?

Hand on throat, say *thigh* and *ether*. They are both voiceless and are represented by the [θ]. On the other hand, *thy*, *either*, as well as *the* and *other* from this (yes, *this* is another one) sentence are all voiced. We need to bring back an old symbol to represent this sound. In an earlier form of English, we used a crossed *d* to represent both the voiced and voiceless *th* sounds. Today, we use the ð (ironically called the *eth*, with the [θ] as the final sound) to represent only the voiced interdental fricative, as in *thy* or *the*. Because this difference is so hidden by the orthography, you may need to practise explicitly recognizing the difference. For most non-native learners of English, this is not a problem; you learned it explicitly. Table 2.2 presents some common words for each of the two interdental fricatives. Note the paired words are similar, but they are not all minimal pairs.

Table 2.2 Interdental fricatives

Voiced Interdental Fricative: [ð]	Voiceless Interdental Fricative: [θ]
either	ether
thy	thigh
this	thistle
then	thin
the	thud

ACTIVITY 2.4

Voiced [ð] or voiceless [θ]? Fill in the blank with the correct symbol for each of these *th* words.
1. _____ think
2. _____ breathe
3. _____ breath
4. _____ the
5. _____ thesis

In later chapters, we'll talk about why the [ð, θ] sounds are so difficult and how to teach them. At the same time, you learn that the **functional load** (how much work a sound does to making language intelligible) for the [ð, θ] sounds is so low that it's not really worth the effort to practise them until they are 'perfect'. We'll come back to that important issue: is this sound really important if we just want intelligibility? But for now, we will continue to move back farther in the mouth on our grand tour.

Gum Ridge: Alveolar

Put your tongue in the interdental position for [ð] or [θ]. Pull your tongue in and up over your teeth until you hit a small ridge that seems to hold your teeth in place. That is the **alveolar ridge** and is important in producing many basic English sounds.

Say the following words slowly and carefully: *Sue, zoo, too, do, new.* As you do, notice where the tip of your tongue is each time for the initial sound in each word.

You didn't need to move the tip of your tongue at all to make those sounds. They are all made by placing the tongue at the top of the teeth, with a bit of tongue touching the alveolar ridge. As a result, we call these sounds *alveolar*. We still have to divide them by manner of articulation (stop, fricative or nasal) and by voicing. Fortunately, we won't need any new symbols for these sounds.

The [s] in *Sue* is a voiceless alveolar fricative, which is paired with its voiced partner [z] as in *zoo*. That then means [z] is a voiced alveolar fricative. Be careful not to confuse the letter *s* with the sound [s]. For example, the *s* in *confuse* is actually a [z] sound. Sometimes, the sound changes even in different forms of the same words. For example, the word *house* ends in the [s] sound, but both *s* letters in *houses* are really [z] sounds. You can't tell by just looking at the spelling of a word; you have to say the word out loud to know how to write it down with phonetic symbols, which we call *transcribing*. Most languages have both these sounds, but even if they don't, it's usually not a real problem for the learners. Not all English sounds that are 'missing' in a learner's native language are equally difficult to learn. For example, Danish, Norwegian and Swedish have no [z], but in thirty years of teaching we've never encountered a speaker of those languages who had problems with the [z]. Of course, you may encounter a PAY context where there is a small problem, but it's not likely.

Although you may not encounter speakers of Danish or Swedish in your classes, if you are teaching or living in North America, you will certainly have Spanish speakers in some of your classes. It may come as a surprise to many English speakers that many Spanish dialects don't have a [z] sound. Did you ever notice that as a problem for Spanish speakers speaking English? Most likely, you haven't. In other words, once again some missing sounds are harder than other missing sounds. If your Spanish or Swedish speakers have no problem with the minimal pair *Sue/zoo*, spend no time on it.

Say this minimal pair: *time/dime*. It lets us determine that [t] is a voiceless alveolar stop that is paired with [d], a voiced alveolar stop. This minimal pair shows us this distinction is significant at the beginnings of words, also known as the **initial** *position*; and *bed/bet* shows the significance in *final position*. We'll discuss later that not all sound differences might be significant in all positions, initial, **medial** ('in the middle') and final. There is another difference between syllable-initial [t] and [d] that can be problematic for speakers of Spanish, Italian, Dutch and French, but we will talk about that phenomenon (aspiration) in the next chapter.

Try the finger moustache trick with the [n] in *no*, and you will quickly feel that [n] is an alveolar nasal. Remember, we're not discussing voicing and nasals at this point, and they don't have partners.

Small Changes: Accents

Although these five sounds [s, z, t, d, n] are common in most world languages, they are produced slightly differently in each language. Say *do*, but push your tongue closer to the ends of your teeth so that your tongue doesn't touch your alveolar ridge at all. That is the [d] sound most commonly used in French, German, Spanish and many other languages. It's much more *dental* than alveolar and sounds a bit 'metallic' to English speakers. Although speakers of French or Spanish would have no trouble understanding your American/Canadian/British alveolar [d] instead of their dental [d], that tiny difference would be one of the major causes of the instantly identifiable Anglo accent.

That means that if you can train yourself to just push your tongue forward every time you say a [d] in those languages, your accent will instantly be much better. It is easy to tell you to do that, but it is hard to break the muscle memory that your tongue has for the perfect alveolar Anglo [s], [z], [t], [d] or [n]. Likewise, if you are a Spanish speaker, all you have to do is pull your tongue back a bit for [s], [z], [t], [d] or [n] to sound more American/British/Canadian or even Australian. Your tongue's muscle memory will fight you all the way, but it can be done. Later in Chapter 5, we talk again about 'muscle memory' that involves much more than just muscles. We call the habitual way you hold your mouth, tense your throat muscles and push your tongue forward or back your basic **articulatory setting**. The prototypical articulatory setting used by almost all members of an accent/dialect/language group has a large, but often ignored influence on the pronunciation of L2. But again, that is discussed more in Chapter 5.

Gum Ridge and Hard Palate: Alveopalatal

We're going to return to this area of the mouth again later, but let's move back just a bit. Say *Sue*, but hold onto the [s] sound as you gently and slowly pull your tongue back and up from the alveolar ridge to the *hard palate*. At which point did *Sue* change to *shoe*? Say *shoe, she, shine* and *shame*. For most speakers the tip of the tongue is not touching anywhere, and the sides of the tongue curl up a bit to form a groove for the air to come through. You remember that the two-letters-for-one-sound combination *sh* in these words is a digraph, so we must create a symbol for this one sound. You need to be familiar with two different symbols because the IPA uses one and many Americans use another. It doesn't matter which one you choose unless your instructor has a distinct preference. Then, you are advised to use that one.

The American version is [š], an *s* with a cap, called the *capped s*. Letters with caps (the cap is officially called a *háček*) are used in Czech, Lithuanian and several other languages. Some linguists call it a wedge. It doesn't matter unless someone says it matters. The official IPA form and that used by most Europeans is [ʃ], which can be called the *esh* or the stretched *s*.

The authors prefer the [š] because (i) they are American; (ii) the first author speaks Czech; and (iii) especially because using that form makes explicit certain phonetic patterns we will see in the next segment. So how do we describe and name [š]?

We call the place where [š] is articulated **alveopalatal** (from *palate*) because both the alveolar ridge and the hard palate are involved. We know instantly that the sound is a fricative. Is it voiced or voiceless? Voiceless, so the [š] is a voiceless alveopalatal fricative. Other names for this place are *postalveolar* or even just *palatal*, but we use alveopalatal here.

This sound is found in most languages; however, in Spanish, it's only found in loan words. When Spanish speakers learn English, they often substitute the sound in *cheap* for the [š], so we hear the stereotypical confusion between *ship/chip/sheep/cheap*. What might be frustrating for the English instructor is that the learner will sometimes say [š] and sometimes not. In other words, saying something 'correctly' once doesn't mean that sound will be pronounced 'correctly' all the time; **learning** is circular, not linear.

Placement and Combination Rules: Phonotactics

Of course, we need to find out what the [š]'s voiced partner is, but we need to discuss one new term before we examine the voiced alveopalatal fricative. While discussing phonetics, we are only concerned with the production and perception of individual sounds, but there is a complication that needs to be discussed here briefly, although we discuss it more in Chapter 3. That phenomenon is not how sounds are made, but how sounds can combine with other sounds and where sounds can occur in words. This new term is **phonotactics**, the arrangement of sounds.

Take for example the sound [h] in the name *Hall*. It can only occur at the beginning of syllables: *Hall, behind*. When we write *Sarah*, we don't say an [h] at the end in English. It's just not 'allowed'. Likewise, the [h] can only come before a vowel in Modern English. In Old English, [h] could come before certain consonants, so we had words such as *hros, hring, hravn* that changed in Modern English to *horse, ring* and *raven* to match the changing phonotactics of English.

Sometimes certain *clusters* such as the [kl] in *cluster* are only allowed in certain positions in a word. We can begin a word with [kl] in English but can't end a word with that cluster. You might think that the word *winkle* ends with [kl], but here the two form a syllable rather than a cluster. On the other hand, we can end a word with [ps] as in *caps*, but we can't begin one with that cluster even if we write it that way, as in *psychology*. Our linguistic neighbours, French and German, allow [ps] at the beginning of a word with wild abandon. Try to pronounce *psychology* with an initial [ps]. It sounds a bit like the second syllable in *capsize*. Fine, we now know that phonotactics describes how languages combine and place sounds (not letters). We can return to the alveopalatal fricatives and see why that detour was important.

Confusion: The Voiced Alveopalatal Fricative

The *voiced alveopalatal fricative* doesn't occur in all positions in all varieties of English. In other words, there are some phonotactic restrictions. Let's begin with a position where all English varieties agree. Say *vision, fusion, confusion*. Even though we write *s*, it's clear that is not an *s* sound in the middle. In fact, the *i* seems to have disappeared completely, and a new sound replaces both *s* and *i*. That sound is the voiced alveopalatal fricative in the medial (middle) position.

If we use the [š] (capped *s*) to represent the voiceless alveopalatal fricative, then we can follow a nice pattern and use the capped *z* to represent its voiced partner: ž. It is clear that the two are related, just as *z* and *s* are. The traditional IPA symbol hides that neat relationship but is used by most Europeans: ʒ. There is a hint of a *z* in the symbol, which is called *ezh*.

The [ʒ] or [ž] doesn't share the same distribution (phonotactics) as the [š]. We can use the [š] initially, medially and finally, as in *shoe, fashion* and *mesh*, respectively. The [ž] only occurs for all English speakers medially, as in *vision*. We can even find an unusual minimal pair to contrast [ž/š] medially: *confusion/ Confucian*. It is not possible to find minimal pairs for the other positions because not all English speakers use [ž] initially or finally.

Any word that has [ž] initially is obviously foreign, such as *genre, Zhivago* or *gendarme*. They don't sound English, and they're not. They are borrowed from French and Russian, which both allow initial [ž] with no problem. The final use of [ž] is a bit more complicated. Say *garage, beige* and *rouge*. Do they all end in the same sound? Is that sound the same as in *vision* or is it the final sound (not letter!) in *edge* or *wedge*? Both pronunciations are acceptable in English although the ones with [ž] are often considered more 'sophisticated'. Again, these words weren't originally English and have complicated histories, but they demonstrate that [ž] has strict phonotactic rules. It can occur in the middle as a modified sound; it can occur initially in a few clearly foreign words; finally, for some speakers it can occur finally. Messy, but accurate. The moral of this story is that we can't just list which sounds a language has but

ACTIVITY 2.5

Let's review the new symbols and labels with a matching exercise.

1. gum ridge sounds _____ A. [d]
2. Spanish [d] _____ B. alveolar
3. [n] _____ C. [ž]
4. voiced stop _____ D. hard palate
5. [s] _____ E. [t]
6. [š] _____ F. [z]
7. voiced fricative _____ G. voiceless fricative
8. capped *z* _____ H. dental
9. voiceless stop _____ I. nasal
10. velum _____ J. [ʃ]

must also determine the phonotactic restrictions a language places on sounds.

Not Always English: The Palatal Fricative

We are going to the top of our mouth and discuss a sound that is used by many but not all English speakers in a limited environment; most discussions of English phonetics don't even discuss it, but it helps us understand how phonotactics and the interaction of sounds are very important concepts in English. This sound is not at all important in itself, but serves as a good example of how different varieties of the same language (in this case English) can have slightly different rules. Say *human* and *huge* with great or excessive vigour. Listen to a partner say the same words. For many speakers, the first sound is the *y* sound in *you*. No sign of an [h]. However, for many other speakers, both *human* and *huge* begin with the letter *h*, but not the [h] sound in *Hall*, for example. For many English speakers, the first sound of these words is more like a leaky radiator or the hissing of a fairly large (non-venomous, we hope) snake than a normal [h] as in *Hall*. That sound is actually the same sound that is used in German (the *ich* sound) and other languages in wider distribution. Notice that you can say that sound without stopping and that it is voiceless. It is a voiceless fricative. Since the body of the tongue makes the narrowest constriction for the air to be pushed through at the top of the mouth, the hard palate, it is a *voiceless palatal fricative*. The IPA symbol is a letter you may recognize from French or Portuguese, where it is used for the simple [s] sound. It is called the *cedilla* and is written ç, a *c* with a comma beneath it; be careful to understand that in the IPA [ç] represents the initial hissing sound of *human* only. Since it's only used in these few words by some speakers, we won't spend any more time on it right now. We introduced it mainly to remind you that the spelling of a word (*huge*) does not predict its pronunciation in many cases and that pronunciation rules can vary from variety to variety.

Soft Palate: Velar Sounds

Let's go further back to the last place of articulation in the English mouth. As you move the tip of your tongue further back, the hard palate changes into the soft palate. You will feel the difference. The scientific name for the soft palate is the *velum* and anything connected with it is **velar**. Let's explore the three velar sounds of Modern English. In a way, they mirror the three bilabial sounds. There is a pair of stops and a nasal.

Velar Stops

Say *cool, kitten* and *chaos*. English orthography hides the fact that the initial sound of those words is basically the same as the one we can represent with [k]. Now you can determine that this a *velar stop* by saying *No kidding!* You can feel that you must stop the airflow completely to say the [k] that you make by lifting the back of your tongue to the velum. Try to say the [k] sound slowly to feel the movement. By now you can quickly determine that it is also voiceless. That means that the [k] is a voiceless velar stop, and it must have a voiced partner.

The sound [k] can be represented by many different spellings in English, as we saw in *cool, kitten* and *chaos*. Its voiced partner [g] has the opposite problem; the letter *g* can represent many different sounds in Modern English. Yes, [g] as in *gone, go, goon* and *ghost* is the voiced velar stop. The problem is that the same letter *g* can also be [f] as in *enough*, [ž] as in *genre* and absolutely nothing as in *night*. However, [g] always and only represents what is inaccurately called the *hard g* as in *govern*.

Velar Nasal

Now we have the stop pair [g, k], and we only need the nasal. Remember, so far we only have two nasals: [m] and [n]. The third and final nasal is becoming complicated in Modern

American English as the pronunciation is changing a bit in much of the United States, especially in parts of the South, where both authors worked for many years and observed the changing pronunciation. Again this change is not that important in the larger picture, but it demonstrates that you must listen to what people actually say (the descriptive approach) rather than assume they use the so-called correct pronunciation (the prescriptive approach).

Say *sing*. How many *sounds* do you hear? In Standard American English, there are three sounds: [s], a vowel and the sound that the digraph *ng* makes. Some Americans now say it with four sounds: [s], a vowel, the sound of the digraph *ng* and then a final [g]. That pronunciation seems more like 'sing-guh' to other English speakers. Which do you say? Remember, as linguists we don't make value judgements about which is better; we just describe them both.

Enough suspense: the sound that the digraph *ng* makes is the velar nasal represented by [ŋ] that looks as though someone fused the *n* and *g* together, which is basically what did happen. It is called the *eng* or the '*n* with a tail'. Just as when producing the [g] and the [k], the back of the tongue rises to the velum to stop the airflow through the mouth, but for the [ŋ], a bit of air escapes through the nose, just as it does for [m] and [n]. However, there is no [g] sound at all when we use just this symbol.

Change in Progress: Velar Nasal

The following will be difficult for some Americans because of the ongoing change in pronunciation. Say *sing* and *singer*. In Standard English, there is no [g] sound in either word. The *ng* is a digraph; it represents one sound. Contrast the word *singer* with the word *finger*. They are not a minimal pair in Standard English. *Finger* has one more sound, [g], than *singer*. You should hear a clear [g] at the beginning of the second syllable of *finger*. These two words do not have the same number of sounds in Standard English. Most English speakers can hear the difference but it is often very difficult for those speakers whose accents/dialects have undergone the [ŋ] to [ŋg] change. You can try also with the pair *ringer* and *linger*: no [g] in the first word, but a clear one in the second. For those speakers who use the [ŋg] form of *singer*, hearing the difference can be difficult. As this change progresses throughout the United States, which it seems to be doing, it will be harder for more and more Americans to hear the difference between *finger* and *singer*. And it won't matter at all because the functional load for the [ŋg]/[ŋ] contrast is very low. It doesn't matter which you say. In fact, there are Americans who just say [ŋ] not [ŋg] in *finger* and in those varieties, *finger* and *singer* do form a minimal pair for the [f] and [s]. Although this pronunciation sounds 'uneducated' to most Americans, that missing [g] doesn't influence intelligibility at all. We hope you've grasped the moral of this story. If your students insist on sticking a [g] into *singer, ringer, bringer* (Is that a word? Well, in any event, you know that there is no [g], right?), and *zinger*, just smile and ignore it. Really, just ignore it for almost all PAYs. And if you have an 'extra' [g] or two when you ring your friend Sterling up to talk about your favourite singer, just ignore that too.

Glottal Fricative

Now we only have a few sounds left before we have the essential English consonants. We said that the velum was the farthest back place of articulation in the English mouth. So the next sound isn't in the mouth. In Modern English, we have one important sound that is made in the *larynx*, or the Adam's apple. When we voice a consonant, the vocal folds in the larynx vibrate just as if we were letting air leak out of a balloon. The space between the folds is called the *glottis*, and the adjective is *glottal*. Say the [h] sound in *Hall*. Try to feel where the [h] is produced. It is in your throat and is basically just 'breathy'. The [h] is a *voiceless glottal fricative*. It is an odd sound, and many linguists have been trying to give it many different names; some even want to call it a voiceless vowel. That is too much bother for us; we will stick with the old-fashioned voiceless glottal fricative.

'Urricanes 'ardly 'appen in phonetics classes: the case of the missing, changed or overeager [h]

You know that this [h] is a sound that is 'dropped' by some speakers of British English and by many French speakers of English. It is also a sound that is difficult for speakers of other languages, such as Russian, who don't have it and substitute the [x] sound that is found at the end of the name *Bach* (German pronunciation) or in the Scottish *loch*, which neither author has actually ever heard someone say, although it's always mentioned, just as we just did, as an example of that sound. That [x] is actually a *voiceless velar fricative* that English once had in words such as *right, night, light* and other words that now have the silent *gh* combination. We assume that you never really thought (see what we did there?) about what the *gh* might (are you paying attention?) have been throughout (another one!) the history of English. Well, now you know, though (!), it might not be the most interesting thing you've ever learnt.

Of course, to round out the discussion, there has to be a case when someone overuses the [h] sound. We'll only give one example but one that ticks off many Americans and even some British people, although not us because we are objective linguists who value all sounds equally. What is the name of the letter *h*? In most varieties of English, that name begins with a vowel and ends with a sound we haven't yet discussed that is the same as the first sound in *Charles*. On the other hand, many British people stick an [h] on the name of the letter so that *h/hate* form a minimal pair with only the final sounds differing. Again we don't judge; we just observe, even if we might be a bit judgemental when no one is paying attention.

Stop and Fricative: Affricate

Let's leave the throat and return to the mouth to discuss two sounds that are a little complicated. When you were asked to say *garage*, some of you ended the word with [ž], the voiced alveolar-palatal fricative, but some of you ended it with the final sound in *edge*. Let's listen more closely to the word *edge*. There are four letters, but how many sounds are there? Almost all native English speakers hear just two sounds: the vowel and the last consonant.

That last consonant is called an **affricate** because it is really composed of a stop and a fricative. It is two sounds, but for complicated reasons, English speakers perceive it as one. If you ask a German or French speaker, this person will most likely tell you that she or he hears a [d] + [ž] because in those languages, that is the way that sound is perceived and used.

Because that combination counts as *one* sound in English, we use *one* symbol, a capped *j*: [ǰ]. Try to say the first sound in *judge* slowly, and you can almost hear the transition from [d] to [ž]. Unlike a stop, the sound isn't quite instantaneous, but unlike a fricative, it cannot be extended. It is an affricate.

You already know that both [d] and [ž] are voiced, so that means [ǰ] is a voiced affricate. And since it combines both [d] and [ž], it is a *voiced alveopalatal affricate*. It must have a voiceless partner, and it does: the first and the last sounds in *church*. You might have already guessed that this *voiceless alveopalatal affricate* is produced by combining the voiceless partners of [d] and [ž]: [t] and [š]. The symbol we use when we want it to be clear that we perceive the voiceless alveopalatal affricative as *one* sound is [č], which is the symbol that the Czechs use to spell their own name in their own language: Čech. They hear [č] as one sound (and it's written that way in their language), whereas the French and Germans again would hear two sounds: [t] and [š], spelled *tsch* and *tch*, respectively. Oddly, the *cz* combination we use to spell *Czech* is actually the Polish digraph for that sound.

Not everyone uses these symbols. You might encounter [dž] or [ʤ] for [ǰ], and [tš] or [ʧ] for [č]. It doesn't matter at this point which you use as long as you are consistent. Again, we prefer [ǰ] and [č] because they remind us that in English these affricates are perceived as one sound each by native speakers of English.

Depending on the PAY, the affricates can be a problem. For example, many Arabic speakers substitute the affricate [ǰ] for [ž] intervocalically (between two vowels). A word such as *usually* will be pronounced 'incorrectly' but can still be easily understood. What could frustrate the instructor is that the speakers may seem to alternate between the 'correct' and the 'incorrect' pronunciation.

Another common PAY involving the affricates is with many Spanish speakers. The situation really is PAY specific, since different dialects/accents of Spanish handle affricates differently.

Approximants

Our final four consonants are important in teaching English to non-English speakers. These sounds are somewhere between vowels and consonants because they restrict the airflow more than vowels do, but not as much as the other consonants do. They are the initial sounds in *liver, river, Wes* and *yes*.

Say those words. Just as for fricatives, you can hold each sound for a long time, but there is no friction. So, they are not fricatives and they are clearly not stops. They are also not like the vowels that only shape the mouth. These four sounds constrict the airflow a bit.

We need a new category. For a variety of reasons that are too complex to consider here, we call these sounds **approximants**; think of them as approximating consonants. We further divide the approximants into two categories: **liquids** and semivowels.

Living on the River: Liquids

Say the words *liver* and *river*. For native English speakers, the initial sounds are very different, but for many speakers, especially of Asian languages, they are just variants of the same sound. For now, let's look at how we produce these sounds.

Lateral Liquids

We'll begin with the *l* sounds – yes, *sounds* – in English first. We could just give you the symbol for the basic initial [l] as in *like, look* or *loon*, but let's go a little deeper to see the *phonetic* (remembering that *–etic* means any discernible difference) difference between the regular and the so-called *dark l* as in *ball, bull* and the final *l* in *lull*. Say those words and concentrate on how the final *l* is produced. Take some time with *lull*, and try to hear and feel the difference in the two *l* sounds. You can hear the difference in the first and final *l* in lull quite easily. You should be able to see the phonotactic rule without difficulty here. One sound occurs at the beginning of words and syllables, and the other only at the end of words and syllables.

As you will learn in the next chapter, the phonetic difference in those two *l* sounds isn't important in English, but the difference is there and is a source of 'foreign' accents for learners whose languages only have the initial [l]. The symbol for the 'dark' sound is [ɫ], an *l* with a cross through it. This symbol is used in Polish for a slightly different sound. For much of your work in English, you can ignore this difference and just use the simple [l] when describing English sounds, but it is nice to have it in the back of your mind for when you do need it and as you hear 'foreign' accents. Let's look at the [l].

How do we produce the [l]? Say *la* and hold the [l]. Did you notice that air flows over one or both of the sides of the tongue? There are some slight differences in the way that the [l] is produced and perceived in American and English accents, but that also is too complex for now. Since the air flows over the side of the tongue, we call the [l] a *voiced lateral liquid* or *approximant*. Here **lateral** means 'over the side'. When we give you an option, we don't care which term you use; just be consistent.

The Retroflex Liquid

The other English liquid is the English *r* sound. If you have tried to learn almost any other language, you quickly realized that the English *r* is different from the **trilled** [r] in Spanish or the uvular [ʁ] of Standard German. Say *ride, rode* and *rude*. How does it seem that you produce the English *r* sound? Say it again, and pay close attention to the tip of your tongue.

If you say the *r* slowly enough, you can feel the tip of your tongue curl back a bit. It 'flexes' backwards, and that becomes **retroflex** in phonetics. If you are only talking or writing about English, you can just use /r/ (the slant lines mean it's not a *phonetic* symbol, but something else you will learn about in Chapter 3); however, if you want to use the correct IPA symbol for the most common *r* sound in English, you must use an upside down, backwards r: [ɹ]. We can then call [ɹ] a *voiced retroflex liquid* or *approximant*.

The [ɹ] is a slippery liquid. In many English dialects and accents, it disappears at the end of words. Consider the Standard American and British RP (**Received Pronunciation**) pronunciations of *car* and *rather*. They are quite different. In many British accents, there is no hint an [ɹ] or only a hint of an [ɹ] at the end of words. Even in some American accents, mainly in the South and the Northeast, the final [ɹ] has disappeared. Notice we use the word *disappear*. That means that the pronunciation with [ɹ] is the older form. Shakespeare must have had a beautiful [ɹ] or something similar at the end of his words.

In certain forms of usually urban British English sometimes heard in interviews and broadcasts, the *r* seems to sound more like a [w] as in the word *went*. In most cases it is a labiodental sound represented by [ʋ]. To most Americans, this pronunciation sounds like a speech disorder known as de-rhotacization (from the Greek name for the *r*) made infamous by the cartoon character Elmer Fudd. Indeed, there is a famous British broadcaster who also has this disorder, but his problem is not what we are discussing. The future of this change is unclear at this point, although it seems to be spreading among certain younger urban groups (Docherty and Foulkes, 1999). This change does serve as another reminder that different varieties of the same language can have different rules and sounds.

The other problem with the common retroflex [ɹ] is that it influences preceding vowels. The scientific word for 'r-ish' is **rhotic** from the Greek name of the *r*. You will learn that there are vowels with *r* **off-glides**, not really a separate sound but attached to the vowel before it. You will learn what these symbols mean later in this chapter, but for now, just remember that the little hook at the end of ɝ or ɚ means there is an *r* colouring to the vowel.

ACTIVITY 2.6

Here is a matching exercise on the new symbols and labels you learned in this section.

1. lateral liquid _____ A. phonetic
2. American *r* _____ B. phonemic
3. 'standard' *ng* in singer _____ C. glottal
4. [ç] _____ D. [...ŋg...]
5. [x] _____ E. [...ŋ...]
6. [tš] _____ F. no longer standard English
7. / / _____ G. [l]
8. [h] _____ H. [č]
9. [ ] _____ I. [ɹ]
10. 'standard' *ng* in finger _____ J. sometimes in *huge*

Semivowels

It is quite appropriate that the last class of consonants we examine before we turn to the vowels is the **semivowels**. The semivowels, or **glides**, are [w] and [j] (think of the German word *ja*) as in *west* and *yes*. As usual, there is a bit of disagreement on exactly which symbol to use, so you may see /y/ as the symbol for the *y* sound in English books. Be careful not to confuse sounds with letters. If you remember the childhood jingle about the English vowel *letters (not sounds!)*, '*a, e, i, o, u* and sometimes *y*', you are already aware that *y* and *w* can play different roles in English. For example, the *w* in *hollow* is just a spelling convention. (Well, if you insist on knowing, that final 'silent' *w* often is the relic of an earlier *g*-like sound that disappeared.) It is not a semivowel and isn't even a vowel, unlike the *w* in *vowel* that is a semivowel. Those examples demonstrate that real semivowels can only occur at the beginning of a syllable.

Palatal Semivowel: [j]

Say the initial sound of *yes* slowly. You can hear the vowel sound if you are slow enough. It is a palatal sound. Since it is a semivowel, you assume it's a voiced sound, and that is true in most varieties of Modern English. That means [j] is a voiced palatal semivowel. As you work with speakers from other languages, you will discover that many Spanish speakers have problems with the [j] sounds because of the phonotactics of Spanish. To simplify the issue, let's just say that they often substitute [ǰ] as in *edge* for [j] as in *yes*. The similarity of the two symbols shows us that there is a phonetic relationship that makes that substitution easy.

Labiovelar Semivowel: [w]

If you say the initial sound of *wood* slowly, you will discover that you move your lips to make the sound, but at the same time, you lift the back of your tongue towards the velum (soft palate). Because we use both places of articulation at the same time, we call the [w] a **labiovelar** semivowel. We can say, in an informal manner, that the [w] is just a slow pronunciation of the vowel in *wood*. In fact, Korean speakers usually must work to produce the [w] in front of that similar vowel sound. As a result, the word *wood* only has two sounds for Korean speakers, not three as in Standard English.

When Correct Just Isn't Correct Enough: Hypercorrection

There are many languages that do not have the [w] sound and often substitute the labiodental [v] for it. In fact, in both German and Polish, [v] is spelled *w*; think of the name *Volkswagen*, where the *v* is [f] and the *w* is [v]. Although, for example, German, Norwegian and Czech don't have the [w] sound, a paradoxical phenomenon often takes place. Where the sound [v] (that all the three mentioned languages have) occurs in English, such as in the word *very*, they often substitute the 'difficult' [w] for the *very* easy [v] and it becomes, yes, *wery*. This is an example of **hypercorrection**, applying a rule in the wrong place. It does show, however, that the rule is being learned, with the progressive aspect 'being learned' as the key here. Of course, it truly frustrates the instructor when the L1 sound is used in the same sentence where a hypercorrection takes place: 'The women were (both pronounced with [v]) very (pronounced with [w]) happy.' It doesn't pay to take the time to explain the problem in most cases. Use the 'echo' technique to repeat the sentence with the correct pronunciation, 'Oh, the women were very happy?', and if the speaker is ready for the correction, he or she will hear the mistake and correct it. If not, just move on.

There are many other examples of hypercorrection, and it works both ways: learners of English hypercorrect in English; English speakers hypercorrect when learning a new language. In other words, all types of hypercorrection are just natural processes in both first language **acquisition** (e.g. the child's

'He goed yesterday' by applying the –ed for past tense rule) and, as we've just seen, in second language learning.

Section Summary

We've finished our overview of English consonants. Our discussions were superficial but were enough to provide a foundation for going further in the next chapters. You have learned that to describe consonants, you need to talk about place and manner of articulation and usually voicing. To examine the places of articulation, we toured the mouth from its bilabial entrance on to the labiodental area, stopping to talk about the difficulties of the interdentals. From there we went to the productive alveolar area to the alveopalatal region with its unequal [ž/š] pair in terms of phonotactics. Looking at the palatal area, we saw the rare [ç] and the semivowel [j]. At the back of the mouth, we discussed the velar consonants and the changing nature of the velar nasal [ŋ] in American English. Finally, we descended to the glottis to huff out an [h].

In terms of manner, we classified consonants as stops, fricative, nasals, affricates and finally approximants that include the difficult liquids and semivowels. Since voicing is so important in English, we learned three different ways to test for voicing, including ear poking, neck 'choking' and head patting. Knowing what voicing is and how to test for it, we can begin our discussion of English vowels, as they are, by definition, voiced in English.

Vowels

English consonants are quite consistent in most of the varieties of English from Northern Canada to South Africa. However, the vowels show considerable variability. The actual number of vowels used depends on the variety and accent of English. For that reason, we'll concentrate mainly on the Standard American English vowels, the vowels that both authors use.

The Quadrilateral: The Vowel Chart

To classify vowels, we need to create an imaginary cross-section of a human profile. If you look at a partner's profile, you can say that the mouth is at the *front*, the neck is at the *back*, and the nose is *higher* than the *lower* jaw area. Using those terms, we can begin by classifying vowels as *front* or *back*, and *high* or *low*. We can then add the term *central* for a vowel that is neither front nor back and the term *mid* for a vowel that is neither high nor low. Applying those terms on a grid over our cross-section of the human profile we can create a 'four-sided' vowel chart (Figure 2.2). Since our mouths are not square, the chart is not square, but reflects the 'weak chin' of most people to form a *quadrilateral vowel chart*. Just call it the vowel chart or even vowel triangle, even though it's not a real triangle.

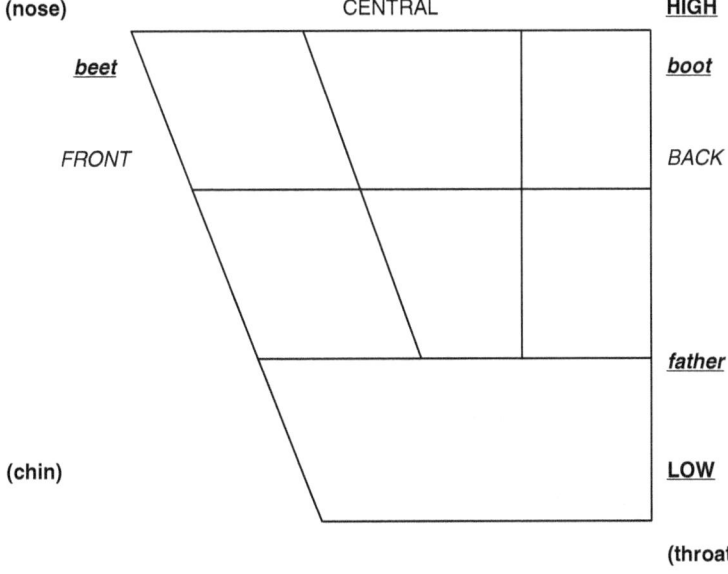

Figure 2.2 Basic vowel chart

Now say the three words underlined on the chart. Concentrate on the vowels and how your tongue and chin move as you say the vowels in *beet, boot* and *father*.

Looking at their placement on the chart as you say them again, notice that you moved your tongue from *front to back* as you went from *beet* to *boot*. Then you had to open your mouth and drop your tongue to say *father*.

Say the trio *beet, boot* and *father* again, and imagine that you are drawing a triangle with your tongue. That is the basic vowel triangle and reflects the basic vowel systems of some languages, such as Cherokee. English has many more vowels than the basic three, and it certainly has many more vowels than it does letters for vowels. As a result, we will need to use IPA symbols again to transcribe vowels. We will use as many minimal pairs as we can to distinguish the vowels, but remember that the way you personally say a word determines how you transcribe it. There is no 'standard' transcription that is universally right, but you can still make mistakes in transcription. It's important that you listen to how you say the word, not the way you think it should be said. Let's look at one example where Southern (American) English merges two Standard American English (SAE) vowels. This is a predictable change that occurs before [n]. In pairs, say the pair *pet/pit*; you hear the difference between the two vowels with no problem. Now say the pairs *pen/pin* or *ten/tin*. In SAE, those form minimal pairs, and there

ACTIVITY 2.7

Front or back? As you say each of these words, try to determine if the vowel is in the front (e.g. *beet*) or back (e.g. *boot*).
1. _____ read
2. _____ rude
3. _____ rode
4. _____ raid
5. _____ rod

is a distinct difference between vowels represented in spelling by the letters *e* and *i*. However, in most varieties of Southern English, the vowels are pronounced identically, both more like *pin/tin* than *pen/ten*.

As before, we will not say that one pronunciation is better or worse; it simply is what it is. We only *describe* the language at this point; we are *descriptive* linguists. In teaching non-native speakers, the situation is slightly different and we must *prescribe* appropriateness; our purpose is *pedagogical*. However, we would never say that saying *pin* for *pen* is 'bad' English. That would be being *prescriptive* especially if we told native speakers what they should or shouldn't do. Instead, we would just tell everyone that's Southern (American) English and smile.

That also means that if you pronounce those pairs identically, when you are transcribing your speech, they should be transcribed identically. Transcription is what we hear, not what we think we should hear.

Remembering that the trio *beet/boot/father* represents the extreme ends of the vowel triangle, we can begin with the vowel in *beet* to explore the vowels. We will use the frame *b_t* with different vowels as much as possible to form minimal pairs, such as *beet* and *boot*. However, before we start, we need to explore two other distinctions that are crucial in describing *English* vowels: *rounded/unrounded* and *tense/lax*.

Rounded/Unrounded Vowels

This contrast is straightforward for the most part in English. Look in a mirror or at a partner as one of you says *beet* and *boot*. You can see that your lips are unrounded for *beet* and rounded for *boot*. In Modern English that distinction is not important because it is actually predictable, but we will still use it in our description since it is important in many languages that we might be learning or that English learners speak. Let's make it a bit easier by giving you one-third of the truth about rounded and unrounded vowels in English: all English *front* vowels are unrounded. Well, clearly that means that the back vowels are a little more complicated, but not very much.

In earlier forms of English, there were front rounded vowels, but they are gone. It would take a long time to explain fully, but the relic plural form *mouse/mice* and forms such as *full/fill* are the modern development of those front rounded vowels. However, in familiar languages, such as German or French, there are front rounded vowels that are often difficult for English speakers to learn. German orthography shows us a bit about the formation of these vowels. You most likely have seen the made-up German word *Fahrvergnügen* used in Volkswagen ads. The *ü* letter in German shows us that it is rounded, like a *u*, but is a front vowel because of the ¨ (called **umlaut**) above the vowel. Now you can figure out that the *ö* is also a front rounded vowel. In French, these two vowels are written *u* and *œ* respectively. We will mention these again later.

Now test the vowel in *bot* (as in *robot*). Is the vowel rounded or unrounded? For most speakers, it will be unrounded. As you explore each vowel, you will need to determine if it's rounded or unrounded. As said, that is easy in English.

ACTIVITY 2.8

Rounded or unrounded? As you say each of these words, try to determine if the vowel is in the unrounded (*beet*) or rounded (*boot*).
1. _____ tent
2. _____ toot
3. _____ tote
4. _____ taught (careful!!! It depends on your pronunciation!)
5. _____ tut

Lax/Tense

In contrast to **rounding**, the **lax/tense** distinction is important in Modern English and is often a stumbling block for those learning English from a variety of languages. Once again, we will need to 'strangle' ourselves to feel the distinction.

This time you should grasp your neck so that the top of your hand pushes hard against the bottom of your mouth, which is also known as the dreaded double chin. With your hand firmly on your neck and the bottom of your mouth, say *beet* with great enthusiasm. Say *bit* with lethargy and melancholy. You should feel a substantial difference in tension. The muscles are tensed when you say *beet* but lax when you say *bit*.

In Modern English, there is usually a pair of vowels that are similar, except one is tensed and the other lax. The minimal pair *beet/bit* shows that the best. We can use a phonotactic description as another way to look at the tense/lax distinction that works for native speakers. Of course, in the early stages of language learning, at least, non-native learners don't have access to the internalized native-speaker rules of English to judge if something is possible or not.

In Modern English, only tense vowels can occur as the last sound in a stressed syllable. In stressed syllables, lax vowels must be followed by a consonant: *bee* is tense; and there is no such word as **bi* with the sound of *bit*; you automatically think the word is pronounced like *buy*. Note the asterisk in **bi* means that the form is either wrong/incorrect (e.g. **goed*) or a form that does not exist in English.

We could also call the lax vowels *checked* vowels, but that is not such a common term. Nonetheless, checked is a very useful distinction that could be advantageous for non-natives to help them identify some vowels that might be problematic. By using the term *checked*, we stress that these vowels must be *checked* by a consonant. The opposite vowels, the *free vowels*, can be the final sound of a stressed syllable, and that actually explains why we can spell the single-syllable (therefore stressed in isolation at least) *he, she, we, be, me, ye* with just one *e*, even though it would seem that they should be spelled *hee, shee, wee, bee, mee, yee*. Because the vowel is not followed by a consonant, the only sound that could be there is the same sound as in *wee*. These words alternate between a stressed pronunciation with the free/tense vowel (*He* stole the book.) and an unstressed pronunciation (He *stole* the book!) often with the checked/lax vowel.

We can spell that small special group of words that way because they often alternate between stressed and unstressed, depending on how they are used in conversation. We can't use that 'flexible' spelling with one *e* for all one-syllable words that end in that free (tense) vowel, such as *fee* or *knee*, because they do not alternate between stressed and unstressed vowels. *Fee* is always pronounced with the sound in *beet*. And the way we spell that *tense* vowel is quite confusing for many. Yes, we have many choices in English orthography: *fee, lea, Wii, receive, achieve* and *chic*; however, all are be pronounced with the tensed vowel.

IPA Vowel Symbols

For many reasons, the vowel symbols that we use for the IPA are similar to the way you would spell the vowels in Spanish or Italian. That means that the symbol for the vowel in *beet* is [i], the lower-case *i*. It is the same letter you use to spell *si* (*yes* in Spanish). We can transcribe *beet*: [bit]. Note that is not the English word *bit*, but *beet*, and remember that the square brackets mean that form is an IPA transcription.

The Long and the Short of It

Many books used in American schools insist that there are long and short vowels in English. They are right, but for the wrong reasons. Say *beet*. Some might call this the long *e*;

however, intrinsic length is not important for most English varieties, so that is a misnomer. In most varieties of English, long vowels are the product of interactions with following sounds. We discuss this in depth in Chapter 4, but just to deal with it quickly here, say *bead/beat*. Do you hear that the vowel in *bead* is much longer than the vowel in *beat*? Let's just say that when a vowel precedes a voiced sound, it is longer than when the same vowel precedes a voiceless sound. We could use the IPA symbol for long [ː] if we wanted to be very precise and show the difference in the vowels: *bead*: [biːd] and *beat*: [bit]. However, that difference is predictable. At the same time, it is important to make sure that non-native learners try to produce and hear that difference between the 'same' vowel in *bead* and *beat* in Modern English. Again, in Chapter 4, we discuss why this predictable lengthening of vowels before voiced sounds is so important for non-native speakers' intelligibility so that their listeners can tell whether they are saying *bed* or *bet*, for example, that have the 'same' vowel.

Beet: [i]

Say *beet* and hold the vowel. Now try to feel where your tongue and lips are. When you say *beet*, your tongue is at the top of your mouth and in the front. That means that the vowel is a high, front vowel.

Is it lax or tense? You can easily feel that it is tense by feeling the muscles right under your lower jaw. You could also find that sound at the end of a one-syllable word, such as *bee*, so it must be tensed. Unfortunately, that doesn't help the non-native speaker figure it out. Now is it rounded or unrounded? Looking in the mirror, it is clearly unrounded. That means that the description we need for Modern English for that vowel is that it is a *high front unrounded tense vowel*. Some people list those characteristics in a different order. Don't worry. Most of the time, you don't need to be that precise. You might talk about all the tense vowels or all the unrounded vowels or about all the front vowels and ignore the other distinctions for the moment.

Vowel Purity

Now say *bead*. Again hold the vowel. Do you notice that your tongue moves a little at the end of the vowel? Well, that is because the 'long' vowel before the [d] isn't really a 'pure' vowel. In languages such as Spanish, French or German, even if you hold that vowel for a long time, the tongue never moves. That sound stays a 'pure' vowel. This movement is predictable in English for the 'long' vowels (that only exist in context!) and therefore can be ignored for the moment. We continue this discussion about pure vowels, vowel purity and what happens in English at the end of this chapter.

Boot: [u]

Say [bit] (*beet*) and then say *boot*. As you alternate between the two words, concentrate on the movement of your tongue. You should notice that you basically just pull your tongue straight back. The vowel in *boot* is a high back vowel, and we would spell that sound *u* in Spanish or Italian, such as in the Spanish/Italian word *tú* (you), so the IPA symbol is [u]. You should be able to transcribe *boot* now: [but]. Try to alternate between [bit] *beat* and [but] *boot*. Since you just pull the tongue back or push it forward, they form a front/back pair. We will see that the other vowels in Standard English also form front/back pairs. Don't worry if you forget at first and say *but* or *bit* when you see those transcriptions. Just pretend you are reading Spanish, and it will come out correctly.

Let's go through the other distinctions quickly. Tense/lax? Putting your hand under your chin and against your neck, you can feel the tensed muscle. (Also we can say *boo!* And since it can end a syllable, that means it is tense.) Rounded/unrounded? Look in the mirror and you clearly see that [u] is rounded. That means that [u] is a *high back rounded tense vowel*.

Bot: [ɑ]

Now practise going from [bʌt] to *bot* (short for *robot* in modern usage). For most, that second word will have the same vowel as *father*. What letter would you use for that sound in Spanish, German, French or Italian? The letter *a*. If we want to be accurate, we need to use the so-called fat *a* for this sound: [ɑ]. If we are only talking about English, we can use the simple printed a, which, by the way, turns into the fat *a* if you make it italic in many fonts. The IPA difference between [a] and [ɑ] is not normally important in most varieties of English. Now if we were speaking Dutch or German, it would be important. So we can transcribe *bot*: [bɑt]. How do we describe [ɑ]? It is a low back vowel. Tensed/lax? Rounded/unrounded?

It is hard to feel the tension in the word [bɑt], but [ɑ] can be the final sound in a one-syllable word, *bah*, or [bɑ] as in the famous sheep sound, or in the informal names for mother and father, *ma* and *pa*. That means [ɑ] is tense (or a 'free' vowel). With the mirror test, we see that [ɑ] is unrounded. That allows us to say that [ɑ] is a *low back unrounded tense vowel*.

Bat: [æ]

Now we have the symbols for the basic vowel triangle, [i, u, ɑ]. That was easy. Let's go back to the front of the mouth and say the word *bat*. Watching a partner or looking in a mirror, exaggerate the word *bat*. You see you have to open your mouth and drop your jaw to say that sound. It's clearly low. You can't get any lower. It is in the front bottom of your mouth. Of course because the mouth is smaller at the bottom than it is at the top; the front is much closer to the back at the bottom of your mouth than it is at the top of your mouth.

We can easily see it's unrounded. Can you feel any tension? No, and also you can't end a one-syllable (real) word with that sound. (The onomatopoeic sheep sound *baa, baa* children learn doesn't count as a real word.) Accordingly, the vowel is a *low front unrounded lax vowel*. It is paired with [ɑ] in the back. We still need a nice symbol for it.

Reaching back into the history of writing in English, we use the *ash*, æ, to represent it. In American orthography, we don't use that letter anymore, but it is used occasionally in British texts, such as in the name *Encyclopædia Britannica*. You can see that it is formed by writing *a* and *e* together. To transcribe *bat*, we would write [bæt]. This sound is rare in the world's languages and will cause problems for many learners of English, as we see later in this chapter. In teaching this sound, the first author calls it 'the beautifully ugly vowel' and exaggerates it (using the word *exaggerate*) to help learners.

Bate: [e]

We have examined high and low front vowels. Let's look at a vowel that comes between those extremes, the vowel in *bate*. Say [bit], *bate* and [bæt]. You can feel your mouth opening and your tongue lowering. Since *bate* [bet] is neither high nor low, we call it *mid*. That means that [e] is a *mid front unrounded tense vowel*. Do you agree with that classification? Use the tests you know to make sure. Since we expect a back vowel to correspond with this front vowel, let's go to that sound next.

Boat: [o]

Say [bet] (*bate*) and *boat*. You basically just pull your tongue straight back to say *boat* and round your lips. The symbol is easy [o]; you can feel the tension and see the rounding, so [o] is a *tense mid back rounded vowel*. That means that *boat* is written as [bot].

But: [ʌ]

The final tensed vowel is neither front nor back. Say *but* and try to feel where your tongue is. It is in the middle of your mouth. Since we used *mid* for height, we use *central* for the vowels that are neither front nor back. Looking at the other distinctions, we find that this vowel is a *mid central unrounded tense vowel*. The symbol is a bit odd since it is an upside down *v*.

It's the sound in *up, judge, mutt, mud, crud, stump, hump* and even *love*. This sound behaves more like a lax vowel than a tense vowel. You may have to listen at first to contrast it with the different vowel in *good, hook* and *book* that we talk about a bit later. In this particular case, the spelling can usually help you. In many Northern English accents/dialects, this sound doesn't exist, and *putt* and *put* are pronounced the same.

Lax Vowels

So far we have examined the tense vowels; remember we said there was a phonotactic difference between lax and tense vowels. Tense vowels can be word final (*bee, bay, boo, beau* and *bah*! or [bi], [be], [bu] and [bɑ]). On the other hand, stressed lax vowels must be followed by a consonant. We will also see that there is a pattern to the pairing. The tense vowel is a lower-case letter, such as [i], while the lax partner is basically a form of the capital letter, in other words, [ɪ].

Since this tense/lax distinction isn't important in many languages, such as Spanish, the tense/lax pairs can be difficult for those learning English.

Lax Front Vowels

We already discussed the three front vowels, [i], [e] and [æ]. The first two are tense and have a lax front partner, but the lax [æ] is the only low front vowel in Modern English. We can look at the two lax front vowels that complete the inventory of front vowels.

Bit: [ɪ]

Contrast [bit] ('beet') and the word *bit*. Put your hand in the lax/tense testing position. You can feel the difference easily. Try to determine if there is a difference in tongue height. There usually is another small difference; the lax form is often slightly lower than the tense form; however, both vowels are

ACTIVITY 2.9

[i] or [ɪ]? Write the symbol for the vowel you hear in each of these words.
1. _____ ream
2. _____ rid
3. _____ rift
4. _____ rieve (archaic word meaning 'to rob')
5. _____ reed

high front unrounded vowels. The difference between them is that [i] is tense, and the vowel in *bit* is lax, so [ɪ] is a high front unrounded lax vowel.

We use a small capital *I* as the symbol so that we can see the relationship. That means that *bit* is transcribed [bɪt]. This distinction is hard for most speakers of Spanish, which only has the tense form. As a result, we heard the standard 'mispronunciations' such as [šip] for *ship*.

Bet: [ɛ]

Now contrast the IPA [bet] (*bait*) and the English word *bet*. The relationship is the same as between [i] and [ɪ]. The symbol for the sound in *bet* is the Greek letter *epsilon* that looks much like a handwritten capital E. Just like [e], the [ɛ] is a mid front unrounded vowel, except it is lax.

We have already explored the low front lax unrounded [æ]. As mentioned, [æ] is relatively rare in other languages. That means that there is often confusion in language learners between [æ] and [ɛ]. For example, Czech and Slovak speakers often confuse *bed* and *bad* ([bɛd] and [bæd]). If you remember the term *functional load* from Chapter 1, we can determine if this contrast is very important and worth spending time on or not. Can you think of many pairs such as *bad/bed* that might be easily confused? It's highly unlikely that we would confuse

ACTIVITY 2.10

[e], [æ] or [ɛ]? Write the correct symbol for the first vowel you hear in each of these words.
1. _____ Tad
2. _____ Taylor
3. _____ Ted
4. _____ mad
5. _____ medical

bed and *bad*: I spent the day in [b__d]. He's such a [b__d] guy! Nonetheless, be aware of this possibility, and if you encounter any possible issues of intelligibility, address them in a lightning drill directly, with emphasis on brief to maintain learners' attention. To paraphrase an English proverb, 'An ounce of attention is worth a ton of tedium.'

Front Vowels

We have looked at all the English front vowels. If you've been keeping track, you have noticed that all front vowels in Modern English are unrounded. In earlier forms of English, there were rounded front vowels, as there still are in German or French, but these no longer exist. In Table 2.3 you can see a simple chart of the front vowels:

Table 2.3 Descriptions of front vowels

i	tense high front unrounded	beet
ɪ	lax high front unrounded	bit
e	tense mid front unrounded	bate
ɛ	lax mid front unrounded	bet
æ	lax low front unrounded	bat

Natural Classes

Looking at the front vowel chart, you can see that there are several ways to group the sounds into different classes (groups) that share a common trait. Clearly, the most obvious class after 'all vowels' would be front vowels, then high or low or mid, or even tense or lax. We can see from the chart that all front vowels are unrounded, so the front vowels belong to the natural class of unrounded vowels. We will see that the opposite isn't true: not all unrounded vowels are front vowels. Using a Venn diagram, we can see those relationships (Figure 2.3):

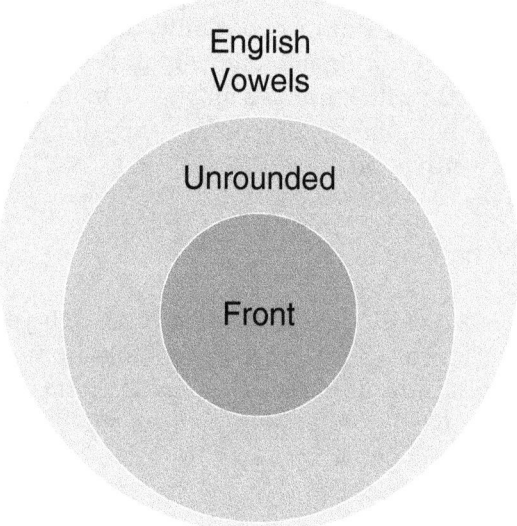

Figure 2.3 Venn diagram with front vowels

That Venn diagram would be very different for languages such as French or German that have front rounded vowels (e.g. Ü or Ö in German). Try to draw that version of a Venn diagram. By looking for **natural classes**, we can capture generalizations that help us understand how language works. Let's turn to another natural class, the lax back vowels.

Lax Back Vowels

We've seen the three tense back vowels: [u], [o] and [ɑ]. In Standard American English, there is mirroring of both the lax and the tense front vowels. That means that there are two lax back vowels that pair with [u] and [o]. Unfortunately, it's not quite that simple because there is also a change in pronunciation that has been ongoing in American English for a while and has upset that symmetry in most American accents.

Book: [ʊ]

Although this sound is completely normal in Modern English, it can still be difficult to distinguish from other related sounds at first. Notice that we had to break the b__t pattern for this sound. Say *book*. Like its tense back partner [u], it is a high back rounded vowel, but it is *lax*. Other words with this sound are *good* [gʊd], *look* [lʊk] and *took* [tʊk]. We use the Greek name of the letter *upsilon* for this symbol although some people call it the 'horseshoe'. Note that this symbol does look like a capital U in contrast to [u].

Bought: [ɔ]

This open O [ɔ] represents the vowel in the 'standard' American pronunciation of *caught*. However, that vowel has changed in many parts of the United States. Many Americans

---

ACTIVITY 2.11

True or false? These words all are pronounced with the [ʊ].

1. _____ look
2. _____ luck
3. _____ buck
4. _____ book
5. _____ soot

no longer have this sound. In much of the United States, the open O [ɔ] has changed to [ɑ] as in *bot*. Try this test to see if your accent/dialect still has this sound. For those who have retained this sound, *caught* and *cot* form a minimal pair: [kɔt]/[kɑt]. For many Americans, however, they are pronounced exactly the same: [kɑt]. Other pairs are *taught/tot*, *bought/bot* and *naught/not*; if they all sound alike, you don't have the open O. This merger is still in progress, so there can be a bit of variety even in the same city and sometimes in the same person. For example, the first author's family name is *Hall*, which he sometimes pronounces with [ɔ] and sometimes with [ɑ] depending on the formality of the situation. Other words that might be still pronounced with [ɔ] are *jaw* or (obviously) *all*, even if *caught/cot* are pronounced the same. Just remember that you should transcribe what you hear or say, not what you think you should hear or say.

Since this lax vowel is paired with the tense [o], the symbol should be a capital O. It would be difficult to tell the capital letter from the lower-case one in many contexts, so the 'open O' symbol was created. Not all English speakers need this symbol, but you must learn it since it is used by many speakers and is part of traditional Standard English.

The Back Vowels

We have now looked at all the English back vowels. Remember that all the *front* vowels were unrounded, so we might assume that all the *back* vowels are rounded. That is not the case. Nonetheless, look at Table 2.4 to see if you can form a natural class that *does* include all the back rounded vowels.

We need to define that natural class of the rounded back vowels in the negative; we must exclude the low back *unrounded* [ɑ]. We can do that by saying that all *non-low* back vowels are rounded. With that, we can turn to the last few vowels that are central in position.

Table 2.4 Descriptions of back vowels

u	tense high back **rounded**	boot
ʊ	lax high back **rounded**	book
o	tense mid back **rounded**	boat
ɔ	lax mid back **rounded**	bought (for some speakers)
ɑ	lax low back **unrounded**	bot

Central Vowels

The central vowels are messy because they also are in flux in many varieties of English. We will use a very simple classification that ignores many of the complex theoretical arguments that don't really help in teaching. For example, you might encounter the 'barred *i*' symbol in other texts [ɨ]; we will ignore it here.

We discussed the mid unrounded tense [ʌ] earlier. It too has a lax variant that just happens to be perhaps the most important vowel in Modern English, the *schwa* (also spelled shwa). This is one of the few IPA symbols you might have learned along the way: [ə]. In Modern English when a vowel is unstressed, it often becomes a schwa. Take the standard example, *sofa*. The final sound is [ə] in English. Even *the* when unstressed goes from [ði] to [ðə]. The schwa then is a *central unrounded lax vowel*.

Butter: [ɚ]

We mentioned earlier that [ɹ] influences vowels that it follows. It is too complex to describe at this point how it influences all the vowels. However, there is one important case we must explore because it is so frequent in English. Say *runner*; how many sounds do you hear? You might expect to hear five, but we only hear four: [r], [ʌ], [n] and the final *r*-like sound. The final two sounds, *–er*, have become one sound, a combination of the schwa and the [ɹ]. To show that it is one sound, the two were merged together to form the schwa with an r off-glide: [ɚ]. This sound is lax, unstressed, and because it has an r off-glide, we call it *rhotacized*, from the Greek name for the letter r. As a result, we can transcribe the Standard American pronunciation of *butter* as [bʌDɚ]. We'll come back to why we use a capital D in American English for *t* between vowels. In many other varieties of English where the final –r is deleted, the transcription would be [bʌtə] (but in this variety, the [t] stays a [t]).

Burt: [ɝ] or [ɚ]

Count the number of sounds in *Burt* as said in Standard American. There are only three, not four sounds as you might expect. If you have a standard British or other 'r-less' accent, you were also expecting only three sounds, but the vowel would be very different from the American vowel. In most American versions, the vowel is basically identical to the final vowel sound in *butter*: [ɚ]. For example, for both authors, both vowels in *murder* are basically identical. However, for some there is a difference. In that case, you could use the less frequent symbol [ɝ] to show the vowel sound in *Burt* or the first vowel in *murder*. However, that added complexity does nothing but confuse people when teaching non-native learners, so we will not deal with it.

The Vowels

We've looked briefly at the most common set of vowels in English. There are other vowels we haven't covered that are only used in some British accents, and even many other vowels in varieties of English around the world.

Putting all the vowels we've discussed together, we have Table 2.5:

Table 2.5 Descriptions of American English vowels

i	high front tense unrounded			u	high back tense rounded
I	high front lax unrounded			ʊ	high back lax rounded
e	mid front tense unrounded	ə	lax mid central unrounded	o	mid back tense rounded
ɛ	mid front lax unrounded	ɚ	rhotacized lax mid central unrounded	ɔ	mid back lax rounded
		ʌ	tense mid central unrounded		
æ	low front lax unrounded			ɑ	low back tense unrounded

Using a more traditional 'vowel triangle', we can also show them as follows (Figure 2.4):

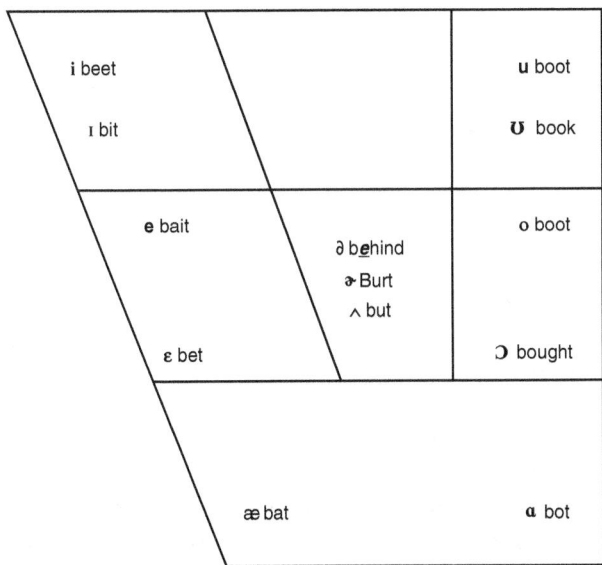

Figure 2.4 American English vowel chart

ACTIVITY 2.12

Put the correct symbol in the blank for the first vowel in each word.

1. _____ eat
2. _____ it
3. _____ oat
4. _____ ought (careful!)
5. _____ ate
6. _____ utter
7. _____ etiquette
8. _____ boot
9. _____ at
10. _____ bot

However, we're not finished with the vowels. We have one final class of vowel sounds: diphthongs. However, practise a bit with the vowel symbols you've learned so far.

Not Really Pure Vowels: [i, e, u, o, ɑ]

Although we call them vowels, the tense vowels are not technically pure vowels in English. A pure vowel is one that only has one sound, and the tongue doesn't change its position. Let's take the two most obvious examples, [e] and [o]. Say *hey* and *oh* slowly. You will hear several different vowel sounds as you extend the word, and your tongue will move around. There is an off-glide into another vowel. If we want to show that off-glide, we use a raised, smaller IPA symbol to show the off-glide is not as important as the main vowel: [eᴵ] or [oᵁ].

It is the off-glide that gives English speakers such obvious accents in other languages with 'pure' vowels, such as

Spanish, French, German or Italian. And exactly in reverse, the absence of the off-glide gives the Spanish, French, Germans and Italians a 'foreign' accent in English.

Technically, we call two vowels that are perceived as one vowel sound **diphthongs**. Since that off-glide is predictable for the English *tense* vowels, we can ignore it for now. Indeed, we prefer not to show the off-glides when we do **broad transcriptions** (that ignore small predictable factors). We do include them in **narrow transcriptions** (that should be as accurate as possible) or when we want to show the differences in the relative length of [o] in *boat/bode*: [bot]/ [bo^{U}d], for example. Say those two words and you can hear the much more noticeable off-glide in *bode*. That vowel is longer because it's before a voiced sound [d]. Yes, stressed vowels are longer before voiced consonants, but don't worry about that right now; we discuss this important and predictable difference in length in vowels later. Of course, there are other ways to represent these vowels and their off-glides. For example, you will see in other approaches to the vowels forms such as /iy/ for [i], /ey/ for [e], /uw/ for [u] and /ow/ for [o]. Again, whatever your instructor or you prefer is okay as long as you are consistent.

On the other hand, there are three sounds that we do recognize as diphthongs because the off-glide isn't predictable and therefore must always be transcribed.

Bout, Bite, Boyd: the Diphthongs

Say *bout*, *bite* and *Boyd*. Concentrate on what happens to your tongue as you slowly pronounce the 'vowels'. You can quickly discover that there are two vowel sounds in each word. However, if you count the syllables, each word has only one syllable. Generally, we can assume that there is one syllable for each vowel, but in the case of the diphthongs, the two vowels create a single unit, and the second vowel, the off-glide, isn't as important.

At this point, we won't add the diphthongs to the vowel chart because they would complicate it too much for our purposes.

Bite: [aⁱ]   Let's look at the diphthong in *bite*. As we say it slowly, we hear [a] and then [ɪ]. When we say it normally, it seems to be one sound. We even have a near minimal pair to show the difference. The name *Ida* has the diphthong and has two syllables [aⁱdə]. On the other hand, the name *Aïda* (from the famous opera) has three syllables and no diphthong [aidɑ]. That means that *Aïda/Ida* shows the difference between having two vowels in a row and a single diphthong. To show that the [ɪ] is an off-glide in the diphthong, we put it raised next to the base vowel [aⁱ]. You will also see it as [ay] or even [aj]. It is your choice, or more likely your instructor's choice, which to use. On the other hand, the two dots over the ï are called a **diaeresis** and show that the two vowels are to be pronounced separately. You have seen this symbol used this way in the words *naïve* and *Noël* that both are pronounced with the two adjoining vowels in distinct syllables.

Bout: [aᵁ]   The second diphthong also begins with [a], but this time the off-glide is [ʊ]. In a word such as *house*, we can hear two vowels if we say the word slowly; however, in real speech, the diphthong counts as one 'vowel'.

Boyd: [ɔⁱ]   The final diphthong and the final sound in this chapter is the only English diphthong that begins with [o] or [ɔ]. It does have the [I] off-glide also. This diphthong is a little tricky since for some people (but not most), a word such as *boy* almost seems to have two syllables. Some poets even cheat a bit with words such as *boy* when they need an extra syllable to perfect their craft or sullen art. However, for most of us, there is just one syllable in the word *boy*.

With the three standard diphthongs, we have completed our overview of the English vowel system.

ACTIVITY 2.13

Now you should be able to transcribe these words with IPA symbols.

1. _____ close
2. _____ loose
3. _____ clothes (careful!)
4. _____ behind
5. _____ gassed
6. _____ receipt
7. _____ TV
8. _____ house
9. _____ house
10. _____ houses

ACTIVITY 2.14

Let's try it the other way. Write the English word transcribed here.

1. _____ [fæt]
2. _____ [ʌv]
3. _____ [fɑðɚ]
4. _____ [frɛnd]
5. _____ [əboᵘt]

Summary

In this chapter, we have undertaken a quick phonetic analysis of the English sounds. We explored the basic manner and places of articulation for the consonants that include the approximants. After that, we investigated the height, position and tension of the vowels in which we also included the diphthongs.

In phonetics, we look at any distinction that might be perceived. In Chapter 3, we concentrate on the distinctions that are significant in English and how they interact as a system.

Suggested Readings

[British English] Phonemic Chart.
https://www.teachingenglish.org.uk/article/phonemic-chart
Although you will learn the meaning of the word *phonemic* in the next chapter, you can still use this chart to explore the different symbols and, most importantly, the different vowel sounds of the 'prestige' variety of British English. Although it is labelled a phonemic chart, it is really a phonetic chart since it shows what happens to the 'abstract' sounds in practice. For example, what in American English would be transcribed as [o] or more narrowly as [oᵘ] in *joke* is listed as [əʊ] on this chart. In fact, you will not find the [o] symbol on the chart at all. To see words that contain the sound featured, you hover your pointer over the sound.

International Phonetic Alphabet.
http://web.uvic.ca/ling/resources/ipa/charts/IPAlab/IPAlab.htm
This interactive website hosted by the Department of Linguistics at the University of Victoria, Canada, allows you to hear English sounds and types of sounds not found in English but that might be used in the languages you speak or that your students speak.

Ladefoged, P., and K. Johnson (2014) *A Course in Phonetics*, 7th edn (Belmont, CA: Cengage Learning).
The late Peter Ladefoged was one of the leading phoneticians in the world. His text remains the standard course book for university-level study in phonetics. Although too complex and involved for our purposes in this book, it can serve as a reference book for those who wish additional insight into phonetics.

Phonetics: The Sounds of American English.
http://soundsofspeech.uiowa.edu/english/english.html
This website is an excellent resource for the beginning pronunciation teacher. Note, however, that the terminology is

slightly different from what is used in this text. An interactive website, it can help teachers learn the basic terms introduced in this chapter. Again, remember that it rarely matters which term you use as long as you are consistent.

The Sounds of [British] English.
http://www.bbc.co.uk/learningenglish/english/features/pronunciation
The British Broadcasting Corporation has excellent resources for learning (British) English. This section of their website introduces the IPA in general. For those interested in learning more about British vowels (the main difference between American and British varieties of English), the lessons here are a good, accessible introduction. They are designed for both EFL and ESL learners but can also be of great benefit to teachers as they begin their study of phonetics.

CHAPTER 3 **Phonology**

> Now that we have examined the sounds of language, we consider how sounds are combined to create phonological systems. More importantly, readers are asked to explore how differing phonological systems influence second language acquisition (SLA) in speech, writing and even reading. To emphasize the role of phonotactics and syllable structure, we use contrastive analyses to explore issues that often arise in teachers' classrooms and workplaces. These examples are part of the pedagogical materials we have developed over thirty years of teaching phonology to language teachers and using that information in classes. Finally, an investigation of how phonetics and phonology interact in English orthography with its well-known graphemic-phonemic relationship helps readers understand how best to help students deal with the written word as well.

Moving from individual sounds in phonetics, we explore four basic concepts that help explain how sounds interact to form the system we call *phonology*. First, we discuss how some sound differences are significant and some aren't by looking at what *phonemes* are. From there, we look briefly at how phonemes are realized as **allophones** and the rules that can be created for *natural classes* that describe in a generalized way what happens to phonemes in various contexts. Finally, we revisit how *phonotactics* describes 'legal' combinations and restrictions of occurrences of sounds in a language.

From Individual Sounds to Systems of Sounds

In Chapter 2, we considered the production and reception of individual sounds in phonetics, and it is time for us to move a little deeper into how sounds are combined to form a sound system: *phonology*. Phonetics deals with describing individual sounds, and applied phonetics helps teachers and students hear and produce those sounds. Phonology and applied phonology are more complex and describe the systematic interactions of sounds in a given language, dialect or even accent. Phonology can be a complex theoretical field, but just as we did in Chapter 2, we are going to concentrate on the aspects of phonology that are most important for second language acquisition and language learning/teaching. Theoretical phonologists would not be very happy with our treatment of their subject in this chapter, but we've included only the information that is useful for the typical teacher to help students.

As we said before, every typical baby is born with an innate ability to acquire any sound that any other human baby can acquire. Remember that babies and young children acquire language. Acquisition is the unconscious act of increasing knowledge, whereas learning is the conscious act. That doesn't mean that children don't learn also. For example, the first author is the godfather of a Czech child who was three years old when this text was being written. During their last visit together, the child consciously practised the rather difficult diminutive form for *godfather* in Czech over and over as they spent time together. The child was clearly learning, but he has also acquired the basics of the complex morphology of Czech that his godfather (the first author) has been learning, not so successfully, for the last twenty-seven years. That distinction between learning and acquiring is important. The three-year-old already speaks 'better' Czech than his godfather, through the power of acquisition, but the godfather knows more words in Czech than the three-year-old, but just barely.

Along the same lines, every typical baby is born able to acquire (not learn!) the rules governing the interaction of sounds for any language to which it is exposed for an extended time. Then, this ability 'turns off' any other possible human language rules that aren't needed for that language; it is an example of the efficiency of the brain. In other words, the rules governing the phonology of every language must be humanly possible. All humans share the same 'hard-wiring' for all aspects of language, and as a result, no language's phonology is harder or easier for children to acquire. Sadly, that is not the case when adults attempt to learn another language; phonetics and phonology can cause many problems for the adult learner.

We could almost say that phonetics is not really theoretical. It is more of a physiological taxonomy of sounds in reference to the production and reception of sounds. At the same time, it is also a physical taxonomy of sounds in reference to the qualities of the sounds themselves. Phonology, on the other hand, is where the physical world interacts with the mental world; in some schools of linguistics, we could say phonology describes the **deep structure** (mental) of the sound system, whereas phonetics allows us to describe the **surface structure** that we hear and produce.

Language Sounds versus Humanly Possible Sounds

What is a language sound as opposed to just a sound, such as a sigh or a groan? Think about the loud, usually vulgar sound made by blowing a large quantity of air through the vibrating lips. It is similar to the sound horses make and is often written as *brrrr* when authors want to include a horse sound. In American English we refer to this sound as a 'raspberry', or a 'Bronx cheer'; it is not polite. If you don't know what this sound is, try first to produce it as it is described below, and then YouTube® it to see if you were correct. You could figure out now, with your new knowledge of phonetics, that that 'rude' sound could be described as a voiceless bilabial trill [ʙ̥] if no tongue is used or as a voiceless *linguolabial* trill if you stick your tongue between your lips when you make it. (The authors prefer the first variety, as it is slightly more polite.) Either way, you would hardly consider it a language sound because you cannot use it to build a word in English. However, the 'tongue-less' variety [ʙ̥] is used in several languages around the world. You can even use it in English if you try, for example, in the word *bright* by trilling (flapping) your lips [ʙ̥] instead of just saying [br]. However, that is exceptional, not typical. Native speakers of English innately know that [ʙ̥] and most certainly the raspberry are not language sounds in English.

Language sounds are the building blocks for syllables that are eventually parts of words. The syllable is very complex to describe, but all language teachers know what one is – or at least think they do. Basically, there are as many syllables in a word as there are individual vowel *sounds*. For example, the word *break* is one syllable with one vowel sound [eᴵ] (remembering that a diphthong counts as one vowel), but there are two syllables in the word *react* [ri ækt] because there are two vowel sounds, even though we spell both *react* and *break* with *ea*.

Now let's look at how innate language sounds are. We can play a game in which we ask you to quickly list four words that begin with the English language sound [z]. That sounds easy, and it may be. You might think of examples such as *zabaglione, zander, zymotic* and *zyzzyva* (yes, that is a real word beloved by Scrabble players). The first syllable of each of those words begins with the sound [z]. We could also ask you to do the same with words that end in [z] or even have a [z] in the middle, as in *raises* [reᴵzəz], which has both a final and a medial [z]. On the other hand, the same game is not possible with the not-so-polite *raspberry* sound. So, you can see that there are possible human sounds that are simply not significant in terms of building blocks for syllables and therefore not for words in *your* language. Of course, blowing someone a raspberry carries a great deal of meaning in the United States, but you cannot build a word with the sound.

These significant differences among phonemes are crucial in phonology. We can even say that phonology is the study of how significant, discrete sounds are 'realized' and combined in each language. We now need terms to differentiate between (i) sounds that are distinct but not significant and (ii) sounds that are both distinct and significant. We will use the suffixes **–etic** and **–emic**, respectively, to describe those two categories. *Etic* and *emic* are terms that come to linguistics from anthropology, where they are used in a similar way in reference to behaviours. Although phonetics concerns itself with the **–etic**, the observable qualities of sounds that can be objectively perceived, phonology involves the **–emic**, the sounds that help create meaning – by building syllables – and are significant in specific languages. Every language has a different set of significant sounds.

Phonemes, Distinct and Significant

If phonology is the study of the patterns or organization of the *emic* sounds in a language, we must be able to write rules that describe those interactions. And that is true: the specific rules of phonology are known by all native speakers of a language at the unconscious level, but the speakers would normally find it almost impossible to explain the rules. A native speaker just knows 'it sounds right that way'. That is, of course, not enough for a teacher or a language learner. And if a teacher were to give that as the final reason to a student who asked a question about English, that teacher might want to look for another job. Learning the conscious explanation of what native speakers know innately relates to one of our goals, which we explained in Chapter 1: to help you be able to explain a bit of English phonology to language teachers, learners and yourself. In later chapters, we discuss more of the rules – which are really just descriptions – that govern how English sounds are realized. In this chapter, we just touch on one or two as examples. But before we can create rules, we have to know what the rules govern.

Phonology looks at the systems of relationships among the sounds themselves more at the mental than at the physical level. The mental representation of the 'perfect' significant sound is the *phoneme*, **phone** + **–eme**. We use slant lines /x/ to show that we are discussing the mental representation of a sound (the phoneme), not the physical sounds; we use square brackets to show that we are discussing physical sounds: [x].

We can find (most of the) phonemes of a language with the minimal pair test. For example, we can easily demonstrate that the sounds [p] and [b] are *significantly* different in English with the minimal pair *park/bark*. Notice that *park* and *bark* differ in exactly one sound, *p/b*. That is what makes them a minimal pair. Don't confuse sound with spelling. In contrast *beat/ beet* is not a minimal pair because they are pronounced the same even though spelled differently. But *wind* (turn something around) and *wind* (moving air) do form a minimal pair because they differ by exactly one sound, even though they are spelled alike but transcribed differently [waɪnd] and [wɪnd]. Those two different vowel sounds belong to two different phonemes. No typical native speaker would confuse the minimal pair *park/bark* in normal conversation. In this case, [p] and [b] are the physical realizations of the mental 'description' of the phonemes /p/ and /b/, respectively. Remember that [p] indicates the physical sound while /p/ represents the mental idea of the /p/. We know from the previous chapter that there is an observable difference, a phonetic difference, between the voiceless [p] and the voiced [b]. And now because we can contrast *park* and *bark*, we also know the difference is significant, in other words, *phonemic*.

A phoneme is the smallest unit of sound in a language that 'native' speakers distinguish as significant as well as different from all the other phonemes of that language. To show that native speakers distinguish different phonemes, we can use a minimal pair, a pair of words that differs by exactly one phoneme (sounds, not spelling) as we saw in *park* and *bark*. Let's give a more complicated example of a minimal pair: *either/ether* (*ether* was once used as a general anaesthetic). Say the two words aloud. Of course, you will have to use [i] as the first vowel in *either* for this to be a minimal pair. You know that those are two different words, but the contrast between the *th* sounds in the two words is not as obvious as *park/bark* at first glance: (i) because we are trained to think of spelling as the authoritative representation of sounds that we called 'hyperliteracy', (ii) because we are aware of different phonemes normally only at the subconscious level and (iii) because there are only a very few minimal pairs for this particular contrast between the two *th-* sounds; in other words, the functional load of that contrast is very low.

As a result of those three factors, few native speakers of English know explicitly that the *digraph* (two letters representing one sound) *th* represents two different phonemes in English, the *voiceless* interdental fricative, /θ/, as in *ether*, and the *voiced* interdental fricative, /ð/, as in *either*. Indeed, we often refer to the digraph *th-* in informal speech as the '*th-* sound', as if there were only one *th-* sound. You, however, learned in Chapter 2, that there is a phonetic difference between these two sounds. The *eth* /ð/ in *either* [iðɚ] is voiced. Put your hand around your throat, exaggerate the beginning of the word *this* and you will feel the vibrations of your vocal cords. On the other hand, the vocal cords don't vibrate for the theta /θ/ in *ether* [iθɚ]; it is voiceless. Now exaggerate the beginning of *thin* [θIn] with your hand around your throat. There is no vibration. There is a clear phon*etic* difference, but is there a phon*emic* one? Yes, because we have minimal pairs to prove that native speakers take notice of the distinction; it is significant.

ACTIVITY 3.1

A minimal pair is sufficient proof that two sounds are different phonemes. Are the following minimal pairs? If so, list the phonemes they represent between slant lines.
1. bad/pad   yes   /b/ and /p/
2. mow/tow   _____   _____
3. went/vent   _____   _____
4. bleak/break   _____   _____
5. breath/breathe _____   _____

Bonus question: A not very careful relative of one the authors has this tattoo: *Just Breath!* Why is that an expected, if tragic, mistake?

Native speakers almost never (except in linguistics classes) need to think about the /ð, θ/ distinction. We can also find a minimal pair where the two sounds contrast in initial position: *thy* [ðaɪ] and *thigh* [θaɪ]. We are confident that few readers will have ever said, 'Thy thigh …' in conversation, but the moment you do, you realize that they are two different words and that the difference is as clear as the difference between *park* and *bark*. This minimal pair shows again that the difference between [ð] and [θ] is significant. In other words, the difference is *phonemic* (both observable and significant) because [ð] and [θ] (square brackets for phonetic symbols) belong to two different phonemes, /ð/ and /θ/ (slant lines for phonemic symbols), respectively, in English.

You now know that there are hundreds of possible speech sounds, but each language uses a relatively small selection of those possibilities and 'turns off' the other possibilities, making learning a new language harder after childhood. This process of turning off the other rules is called the **Critical Age Hypothesis** or the Critical Period Hypothesis. Basically, it says that anyone older than, let's say, fourteen, as there is no single exact age, will ever speak a new language without some trace of 'foreign' accent. Notice it is still called a hypothesis even though the anecdotal evidence for it is very strong. And of course, we all know exceptions, for example the brilliant student who came to the UK at age twenty-seven and now sounds as if she were born at 10 Downing Street, but they are exactly that – exceptions.

Phonology focuses on the limited number of contrasts that each language keeps from the long list of possible contrasts. It also specifies how those contrasts can be combined and what happens when sounds are combined, in other words, the phonological rules that we mentioned at the beginning of this chapter.

We call the collection of significant sounds that are governed by phonological rules the **phonemic inventory** of a language. The most obvious way to determine if any two given sounds belong to different phonemes (significant) is to find a minimal pair such as *raise* [reˈz] and *race* [reˈs]. The threshold for positive proof is very low. With even one single minimal pair, we know definitely that in English there are two phonemes, /z/ and /s/. Remember, when doing this, to ignore spelling and listen only to sounds.

We'll see later, however, that it is not always possible to find minimal pairs for all possible pairings because of phonotactics, which describes how and where sounds can occur and be combined in a given language or dialect. We come back to that term later in this chapter. Nonetheless, we can find enough minimal pairings to build a complete phonemic inventory.

The /ð, θ/ example also draws our attention to something we considered in the last chapter. When we think and talk about phonetics and phonology, we are considering sounds and not letters. Although both are normally written in English as *th*, linguists represent the two different phonemes as /ð/ and /θ/, since the basic phonological rule is one symbol for one sound, and one sound for one symbol. The abstract phonemes are written between slant lines. These slant lines signify a **phonemic transcription** that gives us a representation of the basic sound units needed to distinguish words. Native speakers implicitly know what happens to the 'abstract' phonemes when they are actually pronounced. In other words, native speakers apply phonological rules, so there is often no need to produce a *narrow* (very detailed) *phonetic transcription* when working with native speakers. We discuss that again later. And you now know to call those significant sounds that signal differences in meaning *phonemes*. And by now you may have also realized that *phonemic* means a sound (*phon-*) that is both observable and significant (*emic*).

Since each language has its own phonemic inventory, when someone learns English, or when English speakers learn another language, usually phonemes in the target language are missing in the first language. One obvious example in English is /ð/ and /θ/. Very few languages in the world have either of these sounds. In fact, some dialects of English don't have them either. When people say, 'He da man' ('He's the man', which means 'he's really cool'), they have replaced the rare /ð/ phoneme with the very common /d/ phoneme, which is much more common in world phonologies. Fortunately, there aren't many contexts in which replacing /ð/ with /d/ or even /z/ causes serious communication problems; the functional load of that contrast is very low. On the other hand, the problematic ash phoneme, /æ/, might cause problems on occasion. This sound is also not very common in the world's language, but it might be used in contexts in English that can cause miscommunication. Remember, we mentioned that the **Czech language** doesn't have /æ/, and so its speakers substitute /ɛ/ for the ash. So for most Czech speakers, *mat* and *met* are identical in English, and both sound like [mɛt]. In the next chapter, we look at techniques that are part of the *SeeEnglishSounds*™ system that can help some language teachers and learners to 'see' and then produce the difference between these two common phonemes;

the system can be used if it is determined that time should be spent working on that contrast.

Of course, it also follows that when English speakers learn another language, they will be asked to produce phonemes that do not exist in English. For example, the /x/ sound in German no longer exists in English except in some Scottish varieties in words such as *loch*, although neither author has ever really heard anyone say it in English. The /x/ is a voiceless velar fricative, which sounds very much like someone gargling. You can use that 'impressionistic' information about the sound when you're teaching your own students German, Russian, Arabic, Hebrew or several other languages by asking them to 'dry gargle'. Since /x/ doesn't exist in English, English speakers usually substitute a voiceless velar *stop* /k/ for the voiceless velar *fricative* /x/. Unfortunately, that can lead to some very funny mistakes. For example, German for *good night* is [gutə naxt], but when the English speaker substitutes [k] for [x], the resulting phrase basically means 'good naked', which is not perhaps what you want to wish everyone as they go off to bed.

ACTIVITY 3.2

Because each language has its own inventory of sounds, learning a foreign language usually involves trying to learn a few new sounds. What new sounds have you tried to learn? How did it go? Can you say the new sounds with no problems? Write up a short report about your efforts and the new sounds. For example, since many English-speaking Americans try to learn Spanish, they need to try to produce the Spanish trilled *r* [r]. Have you tried it? If you are a native speaker of another language, report on your efforts to learn an English sound that you find or found difficult. For example, prototypically, most Arabic speakers have trouble pronouncing [p] in any position, so the second part of the name of a common supermarket in Saudi Arabia, Hyperpanda, is pronounced as [banda].

However, even if the target language seems to have the same phonemes, there are still two ways that the learner can be wrong. Phonotactics, discussed later in this chapter, can require the learner to try to use a phoneme in a place that is 'illegal' in her or his first language, such as ending a word with an [h]. And, there can be predictable changes in the phonemes that are difficult for the language learner. We call those predictable changes *allophones*, and begin our discussion of them now.

Allophones, Different but the Same

What happens when two sounds that we can demonstrate to be *phonetically* different seem to be the same 'sound' to native speakers? In other words, two sounds seem to belong to the same phoneme even though we can (sometimes with great effort) find a phonetic distinction? Normally, during first language acquisition, a native speaker produces but then also learns to ignore small (i.e. insignificant) differences in the phonetic realization of a phoneme. These small differences are just predictable information (because they are the automatic results of required phonological rules) that we can ignore in the seemingly endless input we receive in each utterance.

For example, let's take the voiceless velar stop /k/ phoneme that we hear in the words *car* /kar/ and *scar* /skar/. At first when asked about these two *k* sounds, native speakers say that the two *k* sounds are identical. However on detailed examination, we can demonstrate that they are in fact different. However, since that difference is not significant and is completely predictable, the difference is not **phonemic**; it is only **phonetic**. At this point, you also are most likely thinking, 'What? Those *k* sounds in *car* and *scar* are identical.' Yes, they are phonemically identical in English, but they are not phonetically identical.

Try this to feel and see the difference that you may not be able to hear. Tear a long narrow strip from a sheet of paper. Hold the piece of paper with one hand vertically very close to your face so that the loose end of the strip dangles just in front of your mouth. First say *car* with great enthusiasm. If you have done it right, the paper will wave wildly right after the [k] because a strong puff of air follows the phoneme /k/. We call that puff of air **aspiration** from a root that means 'breath' as in *inspiration, respiration* and even *expire* (your last breath). We use a single quote or superscript *h* to represent the aspiration when we need to be more precise in a more narrow phonetic transcription of English, in other words [kʰ] or [k']. We can say that [kʰ] is an aspirated voiceless velar stop. However, in a moment, you will see that aspiration *in English* is contextually predictable and therefore does not need to be specified normally. We can use the phonemic symbol /k/ in the phonemic transcription /kar/, and the native speaker will know automatically in which contexts it is pronounced [kʰ].

Now try the same experiment with the word *scar*, but say the word more gently. This time there is no movement, or at least much less. Alternate the two words *scar* and *car*, and watch the piece of paper. We quickly realize that /k/ is not the same in each word. However, the difference is completely unimportant to most native speakers, except linguists and language teachers. Exactly. This difference is not important in English. Although there are many languages where this difference is important, English is not one of them. The phoneme /k/ is automatically aspirated [kʰ] in *car* and it is automatically unaspirated [k] in *scar*; the difference is predictable and therefore can be ignored by native speakers. English speakers would perceive both sounds to be the same (unless they are forced to put pieces of paper in front of their mouths and puff away).

We call [kʰ] and [k] *allophones* of the phoneme /k/. Their occurrence is completely predictable and cannot signal a difference in meaning as /p/ and /b/ could, for example. These observably phonetically different sounds that are insignificant in terms of meaning are called *allophones*, from roots which mean 'similar sounds'. Each phoneme can, but doesn't have to, have several allophones.

ACTIVITY 3.3

True or false?
1. _____ Phonemes are identical in all languages.
2. _____ Phonemes are predictable sounds.
3. _____ [kʰ] and [k] are different phonemes in English.
4. _____ Phonemic distinctions are significant.
5. _____ Native speakers are often unaware of allophonic variation.

Unreleased Stops

There is another way to pronounce /k/ that can be very important in teaching some non-natives. With great enthusiasm and finality say *top* and then *pot*. You could clearly hear the final [p] and the final [t] respectively and definitely. However, in normal connected speech, we often don't completely release the final consonants. In fact, it's much more complicated than that simple statement and shouldn't even be called unreleased, but that is enough for almost all PAYs. Now say as normally as possible, with no special emphasis, 'Put the top on the pot, Nick' to a partner. The partner should listen careful to the ends of *put, top, pot* and *Nick*. Now say the same sentence with 'unreleased anger', in other words, word by word with clarity. Hear the difference in the ending of those words? Sometimes, it can be hard for non-natives to figure out which word is being said because they are listening for that final consonant. Later you will learn that the relative length of the vowel can be very essential for knowing which consonant should be or is there. For now, just note that the unreleased consonants are absolutely normal allophones, but unlike most allophones, they are not 100 per cent predictable since stress or changes in emphasis can influence what is said. We're not even going to give you the IPA symbol that shows a consonant is unreleased. You can look it up if you need it.

Let's re-examine one other phoneme, /h/, and two of its allophones. Say the word *hello*. Exaggerate the beginning of the word, and you will feel the sound coming from the 'back of your throat'. Actually, as you might remember from the last chapter, the [h] (notice this is the phonetic symbol!) is a **glottal** fricative. That is what we would normally call an *h* sound. However, now say the words *huge* and *human*. What is the first sound you hear? Say them again but exaggerate the first sound. For many Americans, there is a 'leaky radiator' sound that sounds like a hissing of a very large snake, but for others, there is only a *y* sound, as though *human* were written 'youmen' [jumən]. In other words, the *h* sound is completely gone. The leaky radiator (the hissing of a very large snake) sound is transcribed as [ç] and is used in German frequently, but only by some speakers of English in this very restricted context when /h/ begins a word and the next sound is [j]. In this case, we would transcribe *human* as [çjumən]. For other Americans, we can say that /h/ goes to Ø (nothing) in the same context. That means that /h/ can have [h], [ç] and Ø (nothing) as allophones. Usually allophones are predictable and required. Try to say [h] as the first sound in *human*. You most likely said something like 'who man'. It is just not easily possible for a native speaker of English to say [hju ...].

Sometimes it is difficult to imagine that two sounds can be allophones because they sound so very different to language learners. Returning to the /x/ phoneme in Standard German, the English speaker learning Standard German has to learn that /x/ is pronounced [x] after a back vowel (as in the previous example *Nacht* [naxt]). However, after a front vowel, the /x/ is pronounced like the leaky radiator or hissing snake sound that some Americans have in the word *human*, the [ç]. For the non-German speaker the difference is huge, but the German speaker has to think about it to even hear the difference because they are both allophones of /x/ and alternate back and forth under specific circumstances.

ACTIVITY 3.4

In as economical fashion as possible, describe when we use the 'clear' [l] allophone and when we use the 'dark' [ɫ] one. Consider these words: *luck, cool, fly, cooling, alive, Al.*

Remember, we also talked about the two different *l* sounds, [l] and [ɫ] as in the word *lull* [lʌɫ]. They are allophones of the phoneme /l/ because it is predictable when each variant will be produced.

Natural Classes and Rules

Let's return to the /k/, a voiceless velar stop. We saw that it is aspirated when it begins a syllable/word: [kʰæt]. Test that with the slip of paper over your lips as you say *cat*. However, it is not the only English sound that does this. We can quickly see that /p/ and /t/ also undergo the same aspiration in the same environment or context as /k/ did. Use your strip of paper (aka 'aspiration detection device') to demonstrate it. For example, contrast /p/ in the words *par* and *spar* and /t/ in *tar* and *star*. In all three cases, /p/, /t/ and /k/ are aspirated when they are word or syllable initial: [pʰ], [tʰ] and [kʰ]. On the other hand, when those three sounds /p/, /t/ and /k/ follow an /s/ at the beginning of a word or syllable, as in *spar, star* and *scar*, they are unaspirated. That difference is predictable and universal in English. Well, it seems we now have three phonological rules, one for /p/, one for /t/ and one for /k/. However, if we stop there, we miss an important generalization about English. What do the three sounds have in common? By looking at how we describe these three sounds, we will see that they form a *natural class* that allows us to combine the three individual rules in one generalization that applies to all members of their natural class.

In the previous chapter, we learned that consonants can be described using three characteristics: voicing, place of articulation and manner of articulation. That means that we could make natural classes using any of the possible combinations of those characteristics: all the voiced consonants, all the bilabial consonants or all the fricatives. Of course, as you know from Chapter 2, we use different characteristics to describe vowels. Natural classes of vowels can be described by using the characteristics: front/back, high/low, round/unrounded and tense/lax. We come back to forming natural classes, which is very similar to the game 'Which one of these is different?' in many ways, in the next chapter.

Let's now return to the three consonants /p/, /t/ and /k/. What characteristics do they share in common that make them a natural class? As they are all voiceless stops, they form a natural class: the voiceless stops of English. Once we create natural classes, we can see how individual members of a class follow similar patterns in various environments, to produce a systematic organization of the sounds, in other words, phonology.

Using that natural class, we have our first phonological rule that allows us to collapse or combine what happens to the three English voiceless stop phonemes /p/, /t/ and /k/ into one simple statement:

A. Voiceless stops are aspirated when word or syllable initial. Generalizations (i.e. rules), such as A, are crucial to seeing phonology as a system and to understanding how children could/can acquire phonology. They can even be useful in helping adults learn phonology. We look at more rules in later chapters.

Notice that rule A implies (and it is true) that in all other contexts (in the middle or at the end of a word or syllable), the /p/, /t/ and /k/ are not aspirated. We can test and demonstrate that rule. Alternate saying *top/pot* and *cat/tack* (ignore spelling!) and you should be able to hear the differences when /p/, /t/ and /k/ are word initial and word final.

To iterate, these observably different sounds that are insignificant in terms of meaning are called *allophones*, from roots which mean 'similar sounds'. In other words, the aspirated [pʰ], [tʰ] and [kʰ] and the unaspirated [p], [t] and [k] are allophones of the phonemes /p/, /t/ and /k/, respectively. Allophones are always written between square brackets [ ]. These square brackets signify a *phonetic transcription*. In this case, the phonetic detail of the small raised *h* marks a predictable contrast that is not significant and usually only observable if the native speaker concentrates on hearing (or seeing or feeling) the difference.

In the mind of a native speaker of English, [p] and [pʰ] are the same phoneme, /p/, even though there is a phonetic difference between them. If one were to pronounce *par* without the aspiration that normally comes in this context, in other words, as [par] rather than [pʰar], the pronunciation would sound unnatural to native speakers, but there would be no change in meaning. In fact, the native speaker would just assume the speaker had a foreign accent, and that is exactly one of the sources for a 'foreign accent'. For example, in Spanish, French and Dutch, /p/, /t/ and /k/ are never aspirated. As a result, speakers of those languages do not apply rule A and produce unaspirated sounds at the beginning of syllables that seem strange to the ears of native speakers of English. What happens in the reverse situation, when an English speaker speaks Spanish? Of course, the English speaker produces [pʰoko] or even the very 'American' [pʰoᵘkʰoᵘ] instead of the normal [poko] for Spanish *poco* (meaning 'small').

Because each language has different allophones for its phonemes, it is difficult for the language learner to be able to imitate the allophones of the phonemes exactly as the native speaker does. This is also one of the ways social and regional accents develop. In English, the differences are usually in the allophones of the vowels. Think of the different stereotypical pronunciation of the word *my* as used in the very southern American state of Mississippi and in the very northern

American state of Vermont. (These examples can also be heard on the sound files that accompany the text.) You can hear the difference (it is *etic*), but it is not significant in terms of word meaning (it is not *emic*), although it is significant in other ways such as in establishing regional influence and other types of social perception. Of course, we cannot expect the concept of allophone to be that clear cut.

There are also some cases where two sounds that are normally different phonemes might both naturally occur in a specific word without a change in meaning. Take *economics* for example, which can be pronounced with [ɛ] or [i] at the beginning, or *either*, which can be pronounced with an initial [i] or [aɪ] without any change in meaning. These are examples of **free variation**, where two or more sounds can occur in given words without any change in meaning. Normally in English, [i] or [aɪ] are different phonemes and should create a difference in meaning, but in a few words, they do not. This is not a very important topic for teaching or learning a language. For now, you only need to know that there are times when phonemic differences seem to be *neutralized*.

A source of great frustration for language learners is the fact that sounds that are allophones in one language can be different phonemes in another language. In English, the phonetic feature that distinguishes [p] from [pʰ] is predictable and dependent on specifiable environments. In contrast, /p/ and /pʰ/ are separate phonemes in Cantonese and Thai; the presence or absence of aspiration causes a change in meaning. For example, in Thai, [pʰat] means 'stir fry', whereas [pat] means 'to wipe'. If you are a native English speaker, imagine trying to make that difference consistently. Yes, that is one of the reasons why you would sound like a foreigner in Thai or Cantonese unless you happen to be a native speaker of one of those languages. And, of course, the opposite is true too.

For most Spanish speakers, the difference in vowels between *ship* [šɪp] and *sheep* [šip] is very difficult to hear and to produce because both [ɪ] and [i] are allophones of the phoneme /i/ in

Spanish, but in English /ɪ/ and /i/ are different phonemes and are in *contrastive distribution*. It matters if we use /ɪ/ or /i/. They contrast, as would be the case if we put /p/, /t/ and /k/ in front of [__ar]. We would produce *par* [pʰar], *tar* [tʰar] and *car* [kʰar]. Each substitution creates a new word. Although allophonic distribution is completely predictable, we can't predict if a certain phoneme will be used in an allowable position (again, that is phonotactics, which we explore later). For example, we *could* have an English word **har* /har/ but don't yet. Note again that an asterisk in front of a word means it is either wrong or not a word.

The allophones are, by definition, in completely predictable and universal **complementary distribution**. The term simply reminds us that allophone 1 of phoneme X doesn't occur in the same context/environment that allophone 2 of phoneme X does and vice versa. We saw that in the allophones [p] and [pʰ] of the phoneme /p/. We saw that [p] occurs as the second part of a **consonant cluster** [sp] and that [pʰ] only occurs word initial normally. Native speakers of English with no advanced phonetic training would have a very difficult time saying [par] and [spʰar] because the sounds are in complementary distribution, and these pronunciations aren't normal in English.

It should be clearer now that phonemes are the abstract representations of sounds and are the smallest units of sound in a language that can cause a change in meaning. At the same time, there are different realizations of the same phoneme when we actually speak or hear the allophones. We need to speak of an underlying representation of each phoneme, such as /p/ or /b/, whereas the phonetic realization is what exists at the surface, in the form of allophones such as [p] and [pʰ] for /p/. This two-tiered approach is one of the core principles of traditional linguistics. It is one that Swiss linguist Ferdinand de Saussure, one of the founders of modern linguistics, dealt with over a century ago, when he made the distinction between *parole*, French for 'spoken', here meaning the actual linguistic performance, and *langue*, French for 'language', here meaning the abstract system that forms the basis of the language. In some approaches to modern linguistics, that difference is called *surface structure* and *deep structure*, respectively.

A teacher or student of English might ask if it is really necessary to delve into linguistic theory, but being able to distinguish between phonemes is at the base level of understanding for pronunciation that does include both listening and speaking. **Phonemic awareness** is something that native speakers of a language rarely think about explicitly. On the other hand, language learners must be helped to distinguish and try to produce phonemic differences that for them may be only insignificant phonetic differences that they would like to ignore. Some of these differences in phonemic inventories are stereotypically famous, even to the general public. Most native speakers know that many (Southeast) Asians (in the United States, *Asian* is not used for those from India, Pakistan or other South Asian countries), such as the Chinese or Japanese confuse the phonemes /r/ and /l/ in English (e.g. *river* and *liver*) because that difference is allophonic ([l] and [r]) for them (or something right between the two that native speakers of English (NSEs) can't produce when learning Chinese or Japanese). As a result, the language teacher must be able to understand why phonemic awareness is so important to the language learner, and to help the student with techniques which we discuss in later chapters.

Phonotactics and the Syllable

By now, we have mentioned the term *phonotactics* several times in relation to combinations of sounds. In short, phonotactics outlines the possible order and combinations of all sounds in a given language. If you've ever watched the television programme *Wheel of Fortune*, you have seen applied phonotactics. In that game show, contestants win prizes by supplying the correct missing letters to complete specific phrases. For example, if the phrase is _treet_ of go_d, some contestants would be able to figure out quickly what the phrase is. You can use phonotactics to determine what sounds/letters can precede that first *t* and what can follow the second *t*. There are more choices for *go_d*, but the contestants know that the blanks can only be filled by a couple of letters. What are they? Did you figure out the phrase (streets of gold)? Phonotactics at work!

Phonotactics is closely connected to the syllable since it gives the rules that must be followed when building syllables in each language. Let's look at the phonotactics for the /h/ in English as an example. In general, there are three positions in a syllable: the beginning, the middle and the end. There are technical terms for each of them, but they aren't necessary for our purposes.

In English, /h/ can only occur at the beginning of a syllable and only before a vowel (or semivowel for some Americans, depending on their accent and dialect). There is no modern English word *hring*, because the combination *hr* violates the phonotactics of English. However, that is exactly the word for *ring* in Old English, when the phonotactics for *h* was different. Likewise, there was *hravn* for *raven* and several other words that began with *hr*. That is no longer possible in Modern English. We can even also see a change in progress in American English. The *wh-* words (*what, where, why, when* but not *who,*

Activity 3.5

Using your knowledge of phonotactics, you should be able to figure out these common phrases.
1. _here _he _treets _ave n_ n_m_.
2. _paghett_ _nd meatb_ll_.
3. _honetic_ _s g_eat fu_.
4. S_e _peak_ En_li_h very __ll.
5. A_ril i_ _aris.

how) are normally just pronounced with an initial [w] by most Americans, but there are still a few (including one of the authors) who say an [h] at the beginning of each of those words. If you pronounce *which* and *witch* differently and thereby have a minimal pair, you do that too. Most speakers of English don't anymore, and the two words are pronounced exactly the same. In other words, the phonotactics of a language can change over time.

Even though the /h/ is so restricted in Modern English, in many languages /h/ can occur at the end of a syllable or even in the middle of a syllable. Say *hat* and now try to reverse it: *tah*. That is almost impossible for a monolingual English speaker, while the Czechs and many others would have no problem saying it, because the phonotactics of Czech are different. With just that example, it should be clear that differing phonotactics in different languages can cause severe problems for language learners. Even children take time to acquire the complete set of possible combinations. Many family nicknames are the results of a child's attempt to pronounce a combination that the child is not quite able to achieve yet. Perhaps an older brother might end up being called *boo* because a younger sibling could not say *brother* at first. Do you know anyone whose nickname fits this pattern?

We've seen that /h/ can only occur in the syllable initial position as in *hat* or *behind*. There is another phoneme that is the mirror image of the /h/ and can only occur in the final position in a syllable in English: the velar nasal /ŋ/ as in *sing* which forms a minimal pair with the /n/ in *sin*. Remember, this minimal pair shows that /ŋ/ is indeed a phoneme and not an allophone of /n/. Say *sing* and you will hear that there are only three sounds: [sɪŋ]. Now try to reverse that. Although this is not possible in English, in many other languages, beginning a syllable with [ŋ] is no problem. In fact, a very common family name for many Asians is Ng. You may have also seen it spelt as Ing, Eng, Ang and many other ways since clearly Ng violates English phonotactics. Likewise, most monolingual

NSEs are not going to be even close to an authentic pronunciation as they instinctively apply English phonotactics, by adding a vowel at the beginning of [ŋ], so that it works for them.

Another widely known example of this is adding a vowel before a /s/ + consonant to English words by Spanish speakers. The phonotactics of Spanish does not allow an initial *sC* (/s/ plus consonant), so the stereotypical Spanish pronunciation of English *space* is [ɛspes]; *state* is [ɛstet], *school* is [ɛskul] and even *Spanish* becomes [ɛspænɪš]. Did you notice the consonants after the initial /s/ were our old friends, /p, t, k/? Yes, natural classes are important in phonotactics too. This process of adding an initial vowel to 'make it easier to pronounce a word' is called **prosthesis**. This is a very common process in many languages, and speakers of, for example, Hindi and Farsi (Persian) do almost exactly the same things when speaking English that Spanish speakers do.

Let's end our introduction to phonotactics with a brief overview of the phonotactic problems for English learners who speak Chinese as their L1, as Chinese learners of English are now estimated to be in the many millions; in fact, the common wisdom is that there are more learners of English in China now than there are people in the United States.

Chinese phonotactics does not allow any consonant clusters, such as the *cl*, the *st* and the *rs* in the word *clusters*. Nor does it allow any final consonants except /n/ and /ŋ/ (and in some forms, /r/). Just looking at the words in this paragraph, you can see how different English syllable structure is from Chinese. Only one or two words in this entire paragraph are possible Chinese syllables or words. That means that the stereotypical Chinese learner of English has to violate Chinese phonotactics for almost every single English word. That is challenging for sure. Let's briefly look at a few possible English syllable structures allowed by its phonotactics that would cause problems for Chinese speakers (where *C* stands for *consonant* and *V* stands for *vowel*) (Table 3.1):

Table 3.1 Chinese phonotactics and english syllables

Word	Syllable	Problem for Chinese Speakers
feet	CVC	no final consonant in Chinese
free	CCV	no consonant clusters in Chinese
sprite	CCCVC	no consonant clusters and no final consonant
sprites	CCCVCC	no consonant clusters and no final consonant

You can see how difficult the syllable structure of English would be or is for a Chinese speaker learning English. Chinese speakers can say in isolation every one of those phonemes in the examples /f, t, r, s, p/, but they cannot combine them as they can be combined in English. Since almost no final consonants are allowed, Chinese speakers normally just 'delete' all final consonants, making many English words sound almost identical. So for example, *car*, *card* and *cards* are basically identical in speech. For now, you should just be listening to issues that English learners have in pronouncing English so that you can begin to build your own 'bag of problems and fixes' for teaching.

Of course, English speakers experience similar problems when they learn other languages. One of the authors taught German for many years and had to develop ways to help English speakers pronounce an initial *ts*, which we see but don't pronounce in words such as *tsar* or *tsetse fly*. In English [ts] can only occur word final. In English, we can say *cats* /kæts/, but phonotactics doesn't allow /tsæk/. Instead, we would replace /ts/ with [tæk] or [sæk]. Unfortunately for English speakers trying to learn to speak German, this initial /ts/ occurs very commonly in German. Because of a shared origin between the two languages, almost everywhere that English has an initial *t* in a 'short' word, such as *two, ten, tooth, to* or *tug*, there is a [ts] at the beginning of the word in German, usually spelled with the letter *z*. Because this sound is so frequent and not so easy for the English speaker, there might be learner frustration, but fortunately it rarely leads to misunderstanding.

Activity 3.6

Which of these can't be pronounced in English the way they are written because of phonotactics? Why?
1. Nguyen
2. pterodactyl
3. psychology
4. clothes (careful!)
5. mnemonic

We could give many other examples, but we end this chapter with one that occurs in several European languages. In French and German, the initial *p* in words of Greek origin, such as *psychiatry* or *pneumonia*, is pronounced, whereas in English it is just deleted. Again this is not a major issue if communication is the goal, but it is an example of how phonotactics makes pronunciation difficult for English language learners.

Conclusion

In this chapter, we have moved from the individual sounds of phonetics to a basic discussion of four concepts that help explain how sounds interact to form a system, which we now know as *phonology*. First, we discussed the relatively arbitrary way in which a language 'chooses' its *phonemes*. We looked very briefly at examples that show how missing phonemes in the first language can make learning the target language difficult. From there we looked at the realization of phonemes, *allophones*, and started to think about how we can use *natural classes* to create rules (generalizations) predicting their behaviour. Finally, we explored how *phonotactics* describes the restrictions that a language places on 'legal' combinations and occurrences of its phonemes. In the next chapter, we focus on the pedagogical value of this information, in terms of teaching and learning language.

Suggested Readings

Phonology: the sound patterns of language made easy.
>http://www.slideshare.net/richardbinkney/phonology-the-sound-patterns-of-language-made-easy
>This online PowerPoint® presentation provides a good review of what was covered in this chapter and adds a few more concepts that will appeal to those who found phonology interesting.

The linguistic study of language.
>http://wac.colostate.edu/books/sound/chapter4.pdf
>The chapter in this book, available as a downloadable pdf, is very clear and serves as both a review for this chapter as well as providing more exercises and activities for the teacher or class seeking more advanced work in phonological processes in English. The entire book is provided as part of the WAC (Writing Across the Curriculum) Clearing House's open-access books project.

CHAPTER 4 **Research and Pronunciation**

Now that we have examined human sounds and sound systems, we look at the role of teaching pronunciation in major ELT methodologies and approaches. Looking at popular books on pronunciation instruction, we find that some balance a focus on segmental and suprasegmental features (Celce-Murcia, Brinton and Goodwin, 2010); others strike a balance between the suprasegmental features and segmentals, with a leaning more towards the suprasegmental features (Gilbert, 2008); and yet others focus primarily on suprasegmental features (Dalton-Puffer and Seidlhofer, 1994; Kenworthy, 1987). We next survey scholarly and classroom research into producing and receiving spoken language, and identify gaps in the literature, such as the lack of neurolinguistic research into how the brain can be trained to identify new phonemes with the aid of software. Even though this information has appeared in the popular press, it has yet to be incorporated into pedagogical materials. The chapter ends with an extensive look at how best to identify and implement strategies for integrating pronunciation instruction in both the heterogeneous and homogenous classroom.

After having examined human sounds and sound systems, we next look at the role of teaching pronunciation in major ETL methodologies and approaches. Then, we survey scholarly and classroom research into producing and receiving spoken language, and identify gaps in the literature. The chapter ends with a look at how best to identify and implement strategies for integrating pronunciation instruction in both the heterogeneous and homogenous classroom.

Overview

The relative importance of pronunciation in language teaching and learning depends on the current 'right answer' (i.e. method or approach) on how best to teach and learn language. Nonetheless, we can now all agree that it is clear that the relative importance of pronunciation depends on many factors that can be summarized in our mnemonic PAY: purpose, audience and you.

The naïve language learner (as well as the naïve language teacher) thinks that there is but one configuration for PAY: 'I'm learning (or teaching) English.' However, with what you have read so far in this text, you should realize that that is not the case. Each language learning context is much more like the legendary unique snowflake than a clone of some prototypical lesson; each context is similar to others but unique in some ways. And you can already guess that we are going to tell you that different PAYs are going to require different types of research, and different types of research are applicable only to certain PAYs.

In this chapter, we look quickly at the changing role of pronunciation throughout history and in a few of the major methods and approaches (cf. Richards, 2013, for a short read

ACTIVITY 4.1

1. What might be different purposes for *learning* English? Try to list as many as you can, and then compare your list with those of other students in your class.
2. List as many different audiences as possible. You can start with the traditional ESL and EFL distinction and then go from there. Share and compare.
3. What about you? How do you think your personality, skills, training, background and goals will or do influence your teaching of pronunciation?

on the difference in those two terms). From there we see how the little research that has been done on teaching/learning pronunciation has been used and abused when applied to classroom practice. Finally, we offer our own view on how to incorporate the different types of research in your own teaching, bringing us back again to PAY.

Pronunciation, Methods, Approaches and Techniques

Let's assume that it is accurate that human language began with our *homo sapiens sapiens* ancestors around 200,000 years ago. It could have also been 300,000 or 100,000 years ago; it does not really matter for our purposes. What is well established is that writing (as opposed to drawings or pictures) was first developed only 5000 years ago. That means that for the vast majority of humans' time on Earth, learning a language has meant *only* speaking and listening, and that means that pronunciation was most likely important.

Obviously, we have no records of how languages were taught or learned before writing, but clearly it happened; however, again we have to invoke our mantra, PAY, and insist that there must have been different ways of learning and teaching, depending on the different purposes. For example, there are still tribes that practise **linguistic exogamy**. Men must marry (and bring home) a wife from a tribe that speaks a different language. As a result, every person in the village is multilingual from birth. Children learn the language of their mother, the language of their father and even other languages of other men's wives living in the long houses with them. This is exactly what happens in Tukano villages in South America (Jackson, 1983). But this is more an example of multilingual acquisition than explicit language learning.

The purpose (and audience) of linguistic exogamy is clearly very different from the purpose and audience when groups of tribes or peoples develop a *pidgin language* (a simplified form of language that is originally no one's native language) for trade only among themselves. But even in pidgins, pronunciation and especially phonotactics are important, since 'difficult' sounds or clusters are excluded or replaced by simpler sounds. Again there is usually no explicit formal teaching, but in this PAY there is explicit learning and even informal teaching.

Great – people have been learning and teaching languages for as long as people have been speaking. But when did explicit teaching begin, and what was the PAY in terms of pronunciation? There is no definite answer, but it is significant that one of the earliest records we have of language 'textbooks', the Sanskrit *Pratishakyas*, were created about 800 B.C.E. These texts were explicit instructions (teaching) on how to correctly pronounce Vedic hymns. If the hymns weren't pronounced correctly, they might not work. More than a thousand years later, we also find an entire field of explicit teaching of Arabic pronunciation in Islam called *tajweed* that prescribes precisely how the verses of the Qur'an are to be recited aloud. In both cases, 'perfect' pronunciation was the goal for religious reasons.

Clearly, that line of investigation is not helping us much to discuss how pronunciation teaching developed. Rather, let's just skip to one of the first relatively modern SLA writers, *Jan Amos Komenský*, better known by his Latin name *Comenius*. Writing in seventeenth-century Europe, **Comenius** (1592–1670 C.E.) made statements that seem thoroughly modern today. He advocated learning orally rather than through the normal **grammar-translation** method of the day, using objects (*realia*), employing different modalities (such as tactile, olfactory and visual) and a bottom-up approach to learning (examples, then rules) (Rabecq, 1957).

Julius Caesar Is Still Dead: The Grammar-Translation Method

However, Comenius' ideas were never fully adopted. Formal language teaching in Europe and what was to become the United States stayed focused on the *grammar-translation method,* a rather self-explanatory method. The student would read a text aloud, translate it and then spend more time doing repetitive (i.e. boring) grammar exercises. The reading aloud part sounds as though pronunciation would have been important; however, because the languages being studied were the important 'dead' languages (no living native speakers), such as Classical Greek, Latin or Hebrew (dead until the end of the nineteenth century, when it was revived in Europe and in what was later to become modern Israel), there was no need for pronunciation practice.

When modern languages became common subjects in secondary education in the eighteenth century in Europe and the United States, they were treated just as though they were dead languages. The grammar-translation method was carried on by generations of teachers. However, it is only fair to note that the likelihood that a secondary school student in the United States, or even in the United Kingdom for that matter, would go to France was almost nil until fairly recently. In that way, the grammar-translation method was appropriate for the PAY of the context. Learning to read a French novel or scientific article in German was a fine and appropriate purpose. Of course, that means that once again pronunciation was neglected or ignored. And some things haven't changed much; consider that even in the globalized world of education, many (post)graduate programmes in the United States still require a *reading* knowledge or one two foreign languages. When about 80 per cent of all important scientific literature is written in English (Huttner-Koros, 2015), one might think that a rather useless requirement.

Activity 4.2

Our description of the grammar-translation method wasn't exactly enthusiastic. Nonetheless, there are PAYs when that approach is essential. In groups, come up with at least five different PAYs that

> could make good use of the grammar-translation method. For example, the first author works in legal English. Sometimes it is important to be able to translate law from one language to another. 'Just about right' won't do; the translations must be as accurate as possible although the word *accurate* can be a little tricky. Now you try.

Out of the Mouths of Babes: The Direct Method

Around the middle of the nineteenth century, some European philologists, whom we would call applied linguists today, began studying first language acquisition and applied what they saw towards second language teaching. This new approach or method was revolutionary in many ways. Basically, what became known as the *Direct Method* was the antithesis of the grammar-translation method. And with it came the (renewed?) emphasis on native and native-like pronunciation. There was an emphasis on using only the target language in the classroom and interacting with the students for communication, not translation. This approach or method was also called the natural method, but we do not use that term here, since a very similar term is also used for a different method from the twentieth century.

After centuries of focus on the written text, interest in spoken language and pronunciation was becoming more important. This interest finally led in 1886 to the creation of the International Phonetic Association that in turn developed the first reliable way to write about sounds, the International Phonetic Alphabet. The International Phonetic Association also championed the following principles about pronunciation:

- Teach or learn the spoken form before written forms.
- Language teaching should be guided by research in phonetics.
- Both learners and teachers should be taught phonetics.
  (Celce-Murcia et al., 2010)

In spite of these developments, foreign language learning wasn't very successful in most of the still fairly exclusive public (i.e. government) secondary schools in the United States in the late nineteenth and early twentieth centuries. In 1916, the New York City Board of Education sent Professor Carl Krause on an eight-week trip through Europe to study the Direct Method. In his report, Professor Krause (1916) lists five major requirements of the Direct Method:

Above all, arouse and sustain interest.
1. Ensure and insist upon good pronunciation...
2. Give as much oral work as possible...
3. Give more real reading with well-graded texts...
4. Teach grammar thoroughly, not as an end, but simply as a means to an end...
5. Lead your students to understand the life, history and civilization of the country the language of which they are learning. (1916, pp. 14–15)

A hundred years old, Krause's 1916 book deals with the same arguments, contentions and problems that we face today. Appropriately, Krause (1916) begins his description of the Direct Method with an analysis of PAY; the noble statements he makes about the purpose of the Direct Method are still true today:

> But the chief aim in teaching foreign living languages should be to bring within reach all that is good, true, and beautiful in the world, i.e. to be in direct communication with the other great nations... The pupil's national consciousness would be enlarged to the world's consciousness... (p. 7)

Alas, there are two serious issues with the A (audience), and Y (you, the teacher) of the best PAY for the Direct Method, which Krause (1916) addresses well:

- The pupils' attitude toward their school work and home-study is another vital element. (p. 8)

- I can see one danger in this method when followed to its extreme – that personality is too important a factor. ... even the Reform Method [Direct Method] cannot produce phenomenal results unless it be in the hand of a more than ordinary pedagogue. (p. 10)

The method isn't enough; both the students and the teachers must be very motivated and vibrant. Although he observed public (government) schools, we must remember that even public secondary schools were still very exclusive (in socio-economic terms) at the time and provided just the right highly motivated audience and teachers for the Direct Method to be successful.

Motivation, or more accurately lack of motivation, is why the Direct Method was gradually used in its purer forms only in private language schools for adults, such as the famous Berlitz schools. The Direct Method became less effective as public (government) schools became less 'exclusive'. Both students and teachers must be highly motivated. Remember this last sentence, as we will see how forgetting about this basic language teaching 'truism' about motivation can be the ruin of an otherwise seemingly fail-proof method.

Only twenty-three years after Krause's book was published, the Direct Method was relegated to the motivated; in the meantime, grammar-translation regained its hold on foreign language education in Europe and the Americas until the 1940s. Once again pronunciation was almost forgotten, and as suggested in the influential Coleman report (1929), reading knowledge was emphasized since it reflected the actual needs of most Americans studying foreign languages in secondary schools and universities. Notice this is another blunt application of PAY. It is worth noting that even secondary schools were at the time still not really accessible to most Americans; for example, in 1920 approximately 17 per cent of Americans graduated from secondary school. That changed quickly, however, and by the beginning of WWII, more than half of all Americans graduated from secondary schools. And with the 'masses' came a decline in motivation for learning foreign languages.

Parroting the Company Line: Behaviourists and a World War

As Richards and Rodgers (2015) point out, grammar-translation dominated language teaching in the West until a new PAY become important. Until the 1940s and WWII, there was not much need for explicit language teaching for large numbers of learners. Of course, there was a great deal of language learning and acquisition going on, although not that explicitly. For example, there were and still remain a huge number of 'contextual bilinguals', such as existed in pre-WWII Prague where German and Czech were used by overlapping but not identical communities, or as in modern Southern China where school children speak 'Mandarin' Chinese in the classroom and for official purposes but prefer Cantonese on the playground.

However, with WWII came a sudden need to teach mainly oral skills to large numbers of soldiers and civilians, and then the post-war massive migrations of the 1950s brought a need for new methods that produced speakers, not scholars, of languages (Richards and Rodgers, 2015). At the same time, psychologists were exploring different approaches to learn how learning took place and to learn how languages were acquired.

Because the behaviourists (Skinner, 1957) emphasized patterns and repetition, it is not surprising that the major new method was based on repetition and implicit learning thought to be along the lines of acquisition. This method's name, Audio-Lingual Method (ALM), reveals that the oral component was crucially important.

The first author of this text went to secondary school in the mid-1960s with many students who were learning Spanish through ALM while he was learning French and German through a mishmash of grammar-translation and the Direct Method. The learners of Spanish were trained to repeat orally dialogues supposedly with a strong emphasis on 'perfect native-like' pronunciation from the beginning. They were not shown the written forms until after the dialogue had been memorized and repeated ad nauseam.

Then the students were asked to manipulate structures with 'substitution drills'. The teacher would first introduce a basic phrase through backwards build-up, such as, for example, 'The dog almost caught the squirrel.' With backwards build-up, the teacher begins with 'the squirrel' and signals the class to repeat. Then he or she says, 'caught the squirrel' again signalling the students to repeat just that. Next she or he says, 'almost caught the squirrel', again motioning the students to repeat just that (or saying 'Repeat!' in the target language). Finally, the teacher says the entire phrase: 'The dog almost caught the squirrel.' Then the teacher says 'the ball', and the students substitute that phrase in the original and produce 'The dog almost caught the ball.' In this way, students indirectly learn grammar, vocabulary and syntax. At the same time, the instructor also makes sure pronunciation is 'native-like'.

Again, for the highly motivated, ALM was spectacular. Conscientious students could rattle off long, complicated sentences that they had memorized, such as the famous one from a first-year ALM German text: 'I would like strawberries with whipped cream.' For most, however, it was repetitive, tedious and frustrating. The student was more a parrot than a language learner. Open mouth and turn off brain.

At the same time, great emphasis was placed on contrastive analysis, especially in terms of pronunciation. Language labs (with reel-to-reel tape recorders at first) encouraged students to listen to native speakers as models, to mimic them and to practise minimal pairs (such as [bɛd] and [bæd]) to hone their pronunciation of individual phonemes and allophones. Years after first beginning to learn French, the first author remembers spending hours in the language lab, listening over and over to short passages spoken by native speakers and then trying to mimic the contrasts among the four French nasal vowels (even though today many French speakers only use three nasals) in the ALM method. It was more motivation than method that produced an acceptable French accent for the author.

Unfortunately, students could only repeat what they were able to hear and then try to judge themselves whether or not their pronunciation was accurate. Yes, we can train some people to hear, recognize and even produce some new phonemes or other speech feature, but it's not that easy, and it's not always successful (Szpyra-Kozłowska, 2014). If it were, we wouldn't be writing this text. In other words, the three hours that a typical, normal Japanese student might spend recording and then listening to the difference between [ɹ] and [l] is most likely a waste of time, but it's better than doing nothing if you have nothing else to do.

Speaking of wastes of time, until the late 1970s many IEPs still had a separate one-hour pronunciation class. The first author's first publication in the late 1970s was a clever little skit called 'The Bavarian Beer Vendor', written specifically for pronunciation classes, since at that time there were many Spanish speakers in IEPs from Colombia and Venezuela. Using the skit, they could then spend hours acting out implausible dialogue that was tortured prose created specifically to highlight the contrast between [b] and [v] that is often so difficult for most

Activity 4.3

1. Create and carry out a backwards build-up drill for an important phrase for a specific PAY. For example, for a food service PAY, you might want to train future servers to say, 'Would you care for an appetizer to begin with?'
2. Create and carry out a substitution drill for a specific PAY. You need a core pattern and then four or five substitutions. Perhaps you use the basic pattern, 'Would you like more X?', again for the server PAY. Then you could substitute X with bread, water, iced tea, orange juice or whatever might be appropriate for your (imaginary) PAY.
3. What might be a PAY that would benefit from an appropriate use of the grammar-translation method?

Spanish speakers. Of course, we now know that fifty minutes of oral practice is simply too difficult for the average student's productive attention span. The author still quotes from that masterpiece of tongue twisting, but now only for a sentence or two as needed for a teachable moment in an integrated class.

Say What You Mean: Communicative Approaches

Of course, in the pendulum approach to education that we seem to favour (What was excellent yesterday is clearly wrong today!), the ALM method was replaced by methods and approaches that can be grouped together as *Communicative Language Teaching* (CLT). Just as the audio in ALM signalled the importance of the aural-oral, the communicative in CLT tells us that the central focus of these related approaches is to help people communicate in the target language. In reality, there is no single unified CLT method; rather, CLT is more accurately labelled as a set of methodological principles (Doughty and Long, 2003).

The change in method was occurring at the same time that teachers and students both were beginning to realize that the noble but idealistic goal of native-speaker-like pronunciation implicit in the ALM was not a reasonable goal for most. The promises still occasionally made that learners would be mistaken for a native speaker in just three months, or worse that you would speak Language X just like a diplomat, were only true for a very few highly motivated and gifted learners and indeed very few diplomats.

For example, Selinker (1972, as cited in Acton, 1984, p. 71) started using the term *fossilized* to describe the 'fact' that most learners just did not improve, even with instruction, after studying a language for a period of time. In other words, pronunciation instruction didn't help much after a certain point that varied from people to person. These two developments, CLT and the lack of faith in pronunciation instruction, meant explicit pronunciation instruction was not very important in the 1970s and the 1980s. Even today, there isn't much general interest in pronunciation, although that is changing.

With the advent of CLT, the target was communicative *fluency*, not grammatical or pronunciation *accuracy*. Note that here fluency doesn't mean 'sounding like a native speaker', but is something more along the lines of being able to say everything you need to say in a manner that the listener/reader can understand you. Students were usually left on their own when it came to pronunciation. As long as the speakers were intelligible, everyone was happy. Of course, as is discussed later in this chapter, the word intelligible is quite vague.

Even research at the time seemed to say that pronunciation instruction was not very useful. Purcell and Suter (1980) published an influential study that echoed what most teachers felt at the time and many still feel. From the twenty learner variables they studied, they maintained that only four factors were really significant. Unfortunately, those four factors are outside teachers' control, and three of them are outside the learners' control too. For example, the most important factor that predicted success in 'good' pronunciation was the first language of the learner; as an example, they noted that native speakers of Arabic and Farsi had better 'accents' in English than native speakers of Japanese or Thai learning English. And yes, we still think that is basically true; in general, English pronunciation is prototypically easier for certain L1 groups than for others; but remember, there are always exceptions.

The other factors included (i) how long the learner had lived and – *very importantly* – interacted with native speakers in an English-speaking country, (ii) how well learners could mimic what they heard and (iii) how important the learners considered 'good' pronunciation. This last factor, which we might also call a form of motivation, is the only one that could be modified by teachers and learners. Since the common belief was that teaching pronunciation was pointless, it is no wonder that explicit pronunciation instruction was basically ignored for several decades as CLT reigned as the dominant philosophy of language teaching.

The Catch-22 of Teaching Pronunciation

Since pronunciation wasn't important after the fall of the ALM in the early 1970s, pronunciation was not talked about in teaching training courses. As a result, new teachers weren't comfortable teaching pronunciation because they had no training. Since they didn't teach pronunciation, they weren't interested in presentations, articles or workshops – and definitely not in conferences devoted exclusively to pronunciation. There were grammar, writing and cultural-competence conferences, journals and classes, but there was almost nothing being done in pronunciation; that is now beginning to change.

The Answer Is Blowing in the Wind: Renewed Interest in Pronunciation

In 1991, Joan Morley was able to write, 'Beginning in the mid-1980s and continuing into the 1990s there has been a growing interest in revisiting the pronunciation component of the ESL curriculum for adults and young adults' (p. 485). The operative phrase here is 'growing interest'. In the mid-1980s, pronunciation textbooks for learners were being written using CLT techniques. The most famous, by Judy Gilbert (1984), is now in its fourth edition (2012) and comes with audio CDs and assessments. Other classroom texts were introduced and used, but pronunciation classes were still not standard parts of most curricula. Rather, only those interested in pronunciation used them.

In the late 1980s, articles were being written for teaching pronunciation, although the titles often made it sound as though pronunciation had just been discovered. For example, there was a special issue of the journal *TESOL Talk*, entitled 'The Teaching of Pronunciation: An Introduction for Teachers of English as a Second Language' (Avery and Schmidt, 1987). It was almost the end of the twentieth century before there were teacher prep books specifically for pronunciation, such as the now classic text by Celce-Murcia, Brinton and Goodwin

(1996). Even today there are fewer than twenty teacher prep books specifically for pronunciation.

And we are now back to the catch-22; since there are still relatively few teacher prep courses or programmes that offer or require specific courses in teaching pronunciation (in contrast to the ubiquitous courses in teaching grammar, reading or writing), few publishers or authors would commission a teaching pronunciation prep book. The good news is that a quick look at programme requirements on the web shows that the situation is changing. More teacher prep programmes are offering pronunciation classes. That should mean that more teachers in training will be doing research in pronunciation and eventually writing new teacher prep materials, giving conference presentations and even writing textbooks.

Whispering in the Wind: Contemporary Research in Pronunciation

The pronunciation pendulum has swung from the 'speak just like a native speaker' of ALM to the 'why bother?' attitude of CLT and now seems to rest in the middle: 'Intelligibility is a worthwhile and attainable goal.' Of course, just what intelligibility is remains a significant question.

But since the pendulum is still moving a bit back and forth, there has not yet been that much research done in teaching pronunciation in the traditional sense. When we look at what has been written on teaching pronunciation, we can break the articles and books down into two basic genres: quantitative and anecdotal. We can ignore qualitative methods in this cursory overview of research, although they, of course, do have value.

In the academic world, we valorize quantitative studies that have large numbers of subjects and nice control groups. Unfortunately, such studies are practically nonexistent in pronunciation studies for a variety of reasons. Now, we are back in catch-22 territory. Since pronunciation isn't important, pronunciation research isn't important; and because pronunciation research isn't that important, there are few avenues for publishing or even presenting pronunciation research. Researchers (usually university professors) aren't going to research a topic for which there are limited publication opportunities. Getting tenure and being promoted require publications in acceptable journals.

Furthermore, since pronunciation isn't a major part of most language courses, it is hard to create scientific studies with control groups, as might be done for other areas such as reading or grammar. Unfortunately, even if research is done in the traditional control group method, the conclusions might not be applicable to journal readers' contexts that have very different PAYs.

For example, an interesting study on six hours of focused instruction in teaching Mandarin Chinese tones (a difficult and crucial part of learning to pronounce and listen to Chinese) to a mixed L1 class demonstrated better results with the addition of real-time computer-generated visuals than occurred in the control group that did not receive the computer assistance (Wang, 2012); unfortunately, perhaps no English course could devote six hours of instruction time to any one feature. At the end, we are left to wonder if a few minutes or even an hour of CALL instruction will be beneficial for our needs.

Also, as we remember from the depressing article by Purcell and Suter (1980), the three most important factors for 'good' accents cannot be influenced by instruction. Even more significantly, since their single most important factor was the learner's L1, results of studies that focus on speakers of a different L1 might not be applicable. What works for Poles (such as an interesting study with a control group by Święciński, 2006) might not work for neighbouring Germans.

The situation is even more complex in the traditionally heterogeneous ESL class in the United States. There, each student might have a different L1, making traditional quantitative, transferable research extremely difficult. Take, for example, Wang's (2012) study on the teaching of tones; we would have to look carefully at the composition of both groups to see if the results Professor Wang received might not have been actually due to the L1s of the different groups.

'Well, in My Class...': Anecdotal Evidence in Pronunciation Teaching

Sadly, much of what has been written about pronunciation falls in the realm of the anecdotal, basically sharing what worked (or didn't work) for you last semester when you were teaching that nice group from the Central African Republic. The problem with anecdotal evidence is *you*, quite literally. The *Y* in PAY reminds us that every teacher is different and has different skills and weaknesses. Many of the miracle cures for language teaching are the result of one *Y* (teacher) finding techniques, approaches, methods or whatever that work exceptionally well for that particular teacher and that particular group. Almost instantly, the creator of this wonder cure for bad pronunciation heralds it as the answer to all our woes. Well, sometimes these designer methods do work for many people, and the disciples of the method (i.e. those for whom it works well) begin to spread the joyous news. For example, the first author taught (and was required) to teach German through a rather happy drill-sergeant approach called the **Rassias Method** for a year or so in the late 1970s (Rassias Foundation, 1975). He was quite successful with it and still uses some of the techniques decades later. Note carefully the phrase *some of the techniques*. The method (really more a collection of techniques) is very effective in the hands, mouth and brain of the right teacher and with the right audience; this method was created by a brilliant language teacher, Professor John Rassias, who died in 2015 and who left behind beautiful YouTube® videos of some of the best language classes the world has ever experienced in our opinion. But not every *Y* in PAY is the same.

At the same time that the first author was teaching German through the Rassias Method, he took first-semester Russian from a wonderful, but extremely highly-strung, young Russian woman who had somehow made her way from the then Soviet Union to a teaching position that required her to also use the Rassias Method. This novice Russian teacher tried and tried, but with every attempt to exude energy, warmth and humanness, as the website says the method embodies, she simply became increasingly frustrated, shrill and seemingly confrontational. Someone cried in the class almost every day. At the end of the term, her contract to teach was not renewed, not because she was necessarily a bad teacher (or person), but because she was the wrong Y (teacher) for that method. By the way, you have just read an example of anecdotal experience with a method.

In this way, the anecdotal experience of a teacher can be both illuminating and frustrating. Both authors have done teacher training for new teachers. As the trainees observe talented, experienced teachers, the trainees are asked to reflect on a very important question: 'Would that work for *me*? Could I do that?' And many times the answer is no. For example, both authors have seen spectacular lessons involving singing, chanting and even dancing, but they both know that those are not methods that work for them. Nonetheless, they both dutifully attend (anecdotal) workshops, presentation, plenaries and chats that proclaim the universal benefits of those methods so that they can share them with their trainees who might be able to use them. But they themselves never use them (successfully).

Likewise, the first author is positive that he has created an approach he calls *SeeItSayIt English*™ that will revolutionize the pronunciation world, but fortunately, the second author

Activity 4.4

> Think of a specific PAY but let's make the *Y* you. For example, you are teaching low-literacy, adult speakers of Haitian Creole, who work in the service industry in Miami, Florida. Now, using your PAY, what types of activities do you think will work with them? What will work for you? Are you comfortable singing? Would they like group activities? Compare your results with those of your class to see if everyone agrees with your assessment of your unique PAY.

keeps reminding him that nothing works for everybody. That is the problem with anecdotal articles, presentations, methods and even books. You are the only person who can decide what kind of a *Y* you are in the PAY.

Explosions and Expositions: The Twenty-first Century and Pronunciation Research

We have been teaching and learning pronunciation in one way or another for over 100,000 years, and most teachers are still not clear on what they should be teaching. In fact, they're not even sure when, how or if they should be teaching (Foote, Holtby and Derwing, 2011). Fortunately, that seems to be changing.

In the past twenty or so years, there has been a mini-explosion in research and growing interest in pronunciation. There is finally a journal devoted to teaching pronunciation and the eighth iteration of the Pronunciation in Second Language Learning and Teaching Conference (PSLLT) was held in August 2016. Both of these significant efforts are due to the same small group of dedicated researchers and teachers who have brought the question of intelligibility and pronunciation to the mainstream of our profession.

Significantly, there have been several articles and even books that try to apply recent research to classroom practices (Derwing and Munro, 2015; Grant and Brinton, 2014; Reed and Levis, 2015). These researchers have attempted to pull together the often seemingly contradictory research to provide guidelines and so-called best practices. We really dislike the term *best practices* because it seems as though there is a single best practice when, in reality, there are many appropriate practices that match different PAYs. However, the practices they discuss are applicable in many cases.

Before we pull together rather concisely what seems to have been learned by admittedly limited research of over a hundred years of pronunciation research, let's explore the singular most important feature of current approaches to pronunciation: *intelligibility*.

Of course, there is controversy about the exact meaning of intelligibility; nonetheless, we will accept the basic definition used by one of the most prolific and influential researchers in this area, Tracey Derwing (Taylor de Caballero, 2015). Intelligibility is simply how much the *listener* understands. It's interesting that this key term is defined in terms of the listener, not the speaker, but that is right in line with the current emphasis on communicative acts, not mimicry of native-speaker accents.

The companion term, also defined by Derwing, is **comprehensibility**, which is about how much work the listener has to do to understand the speaker. As Taylor de Cabello explains, intelligibility is about the message, whereas comprehensibility is about the listener's experience and emotions (2015). Many tend to think that these terms seem to avoid the native speaker, but that is not true in the world of World Englishes that we explore in Chapter 6. Even in the 'mainstream' English-speaking countries, there are still issues of intelligibility. For example, as a result of the local dialect or accent, there are native speakers of English in the authors' hometown of Memphis, Tennessee, whom the authors can't understand, leading to frustration and dismay on both sides.

The notion of intelligibility has had a major influence on pronunciation teaching if (and only if) our PAY is not 'pass for a native speaker of language X'. And since most of our PAYs these days are based on communication, we accept that various levels of intelligibility are our goal. Once we go beyond the 'pass for native speaker' goal, we can begin to make rational decisions on what to emphasize and make explicit in our teaching.

For example, just quickly listening to certain American and Irish accents, we easily learn that the 'correct' pronunciation of [θ] and [ð] is not at all necessary for complete intelligibility. When American fans of the New Orleans (American) football team, the Saints, fill the stadium with their chant of 'Who dat? Who dat? Who dat say dey gonna beat dem Saints?', there is absolutely no loss of intelligibility, but just in case you don't follow American football, the chant is 'Who's that? Who's that? Who's that that says they are going to beat them [sic] Saints?' Did you understand it?

Most certainly we would notice the *dat* (that) in the Saints' example, but there is no reason to spend time trying to correct what doesn't hinder communication. This modern truth should come as a relief to many non-native teachers who speak perfectly fluent, intelligible English with L1 influences or even to native EFL/ESL teachers who are not speakers of the prestige accent of their region. That was not the case about fifty years ago, when the first author, a speaker of standard American, was in a German-medium boys' school in Germany. During English lessons, he would often roll his eyes as the German teachers of English worked hard to teach the boys [θ] and [ð], even though the teachers themselves couldn't say the sounds 'correctly' either. Sadly, that was before the days when teachers could admit their accent wasn't 'native' and might have asked the American to model the sound or just not bother with excessive work on the troublesome but not very important sounds.

That last example shows the second new truth about pronunciation and intelligibility. Just because the German teachers couldn't say [θ] and [ð] does not mean much time needed to be spent on 'correcting' that problem, either for the teachers or the students. The same was true later, when the first author was teaching German at university. Even with his careful coaching and appropriate techniques, he was unable to help some Americans learn to pronounce the German [ʁ] (*r* sound) reliably in conversation. And yes, although one good American [ɹ] in a perfectly grammatical German sentence does announce loudly, 'This person is an American', it is not essential to spend hours trying to change that sound. It's a waste of time that could be spent on more significant features that can affect intelligibility (and comprehensibility).

Finally, we can look to researchers for help to determine which features do indeed hinder communication the most. We need to ask what features make American English difficult for some L2 listeners or what aspects of Indian English are causing many firms to move their customer service and other business process outsourcing (BPO) work from India to the Philippines (Friginal, 2009, p. 294). This is a crucial issue in World Englishes, where speakers of all types of English must interact and communicate and where intelligibility is the most important single aspect of pronunciation. In Chapter 6, we discuss several researchers' attempts to delimit the core phonological features that must be present to facilitate intelligibility.

Some work has been done determining which features are more important and should serve to help instructors choose where to spend time. For example, in 1987 Catford introduced the term (relative) *functional load* to describe which contrasts are important in terms of intelligibility in English. If there are many common pairs of words that are distinguished by a phonemic contrast (such as the Arabic speaker's shibboleth [p/b]), that pair has a high functional load. And indeed, the functional load for initial *p/b* is 98 per cent from 100 per cent: *pay/bay, park/bark, pig/big*. On the other hand, the functional load for the final *p/b* contrast was calculated by Catford to be only 14 per cent (1987). In fact, it took the authors much longer to find even one example of a pair of words that might be confused: *cup/cub*. In comparison, the rare pair v/ð is only 1 per cent, but we will leave it to the readers to find a potentially confusing pair. Good luck.

Pulling those examples together, we can agree with what Taylor de Caballero learned from Professor Derwing (2015):

1. Some features of an L2 accent have no effect on intelligibility.
2. Not everything we notice needs to be fixed.
3. Research can help us determine which features influence intelligibility the most.

To those three important statements, we can add several more modern 'truths' listed by Donna Brinton (one of the most important figures in pronunciation today) in the epilogue to Linda Grant and Donna Brinton's edited collection *Pronunciation Myths: Applying Second Language Research to Classroom Teaching* (2014). In many ways, most of these research findings support what we are doing. If we add four of her truths with the three above, we have a basic statement of belief about teaching pronunciation today:

4. Most adults will not learn to speak a new language without a 'foreign' accent.
5. Learning to speak (i.e., literally, *pronounce*) an L2 takes more than just cognitive ability and is therefore very different from learning reading, grammar or vocabulary, or even listening. It's physical in addition to cognitive.
6. (Brief) targeted feedback ('correction') is what works best.
7. Learners need to hear authentic language too.

To those seven facts, we can add observations that go all the way back to Purcell and Suter's (1980) article:

8. The L1 of a speaker has major influences on success in pronouncing an L2.
9. Many of the most important factors that influence success are outside the control of the teacher and the learner.

And then, finally, we will add our own tenth and final pearl of great wisdom:

10. It all depends on the PAY.

You should notice that all ten of those 'truths' involve a shift from the goal of sounding native-speaker-like (or perhaps even 'native-speaker-lite'?) to a more realistic goal of intelligible pronunciation.

Once we accept those ten statements as valid, important and correct (for right now), we can also consider other aspects of pronunciation teaching that can be dismissed or supported through research. Let's begin with the so-called '**accent reduction**' issue. Everyone has an accent; the two authors both have American accents. Both have American accents in their spoken Spanish, even though the second author's Spanish is very fluent while the first author sounds like an escapee from a failed teaching experiment. And that is just fine. It is literally impossible to 'reduce' an accent; accents can only be modified. We should only speak of **accent modification**. Thomson (2012) points out that the term *accent reduction*, with its implied negative connotation, is usually used by businesses and that any perceived need for so-called *accent reduction* is usually declared necessary by the very people trying to sell such products (Thomson, 2014).

We also need to help learners decide whether effort should be spent on modifying an accent by looking at their purpose, motivation and even budget. For example, the American Speech and Hearing Association, which also prefers the term *accent modification*, writes about several different reasons for modifying an accent; some involve intelligibility; some, comprehensibility; and some, identity:

- People don't understand you – intelligibility
- People pay more attention to your accent than to what you are saying – comprehensibility and sometimes identity
- You hate having to repeat yourself constantly – intelligibility and comprehensibility
- You want to sound less foreign for regional, professional or social reasons – identity (American Speech-Language-Hearing Association, n.d.)

And now, with accent modification and intelligibility discussed, we can return to what research can do for us. One of the best overviews of what we have learned from research is the short paper that was part of the second PSLLT conference (Darcy, Ewert and Lidster, 2012) and which was then explored more by Darcy (2015). Its authors first outlined the problems:

- What, when and how should we teach?
- How do we emphasize both production and perception?
- How can we help students use what they learn in controlled (in-class) practice in real communication when they are more concerned about meaning? (This is called *carry-over*.)
- What should we teach at different levels of proficiency? (p. 94)

Then, using a review of what we have learned from research, Darcy et al. provide us with crucial principles that should be followed in building curricula that include appropriate pronunciation components.

1. We should use research to help us select which features to focus on.
2. We should address both production and perception.
3. We should begin working on pronunciation even at the low levels of proficiency.
4. We should embed pronunciation in the curriculum and the lesson. We should not have a separate pronunciation class (in most cases, we might add).
5. We should adapt what and how we teach for different levels (and for different groups, we might add).
6. We must continue to develop as pronunciation teachers. (p. 95)

Notice that they don't say 'always includes this feature or that feature', but rather 'select the right element for different PAYs'. With those guidelines then, your job, whether you are interested or not in pronunciation in its own right, will be to continue to learn and update your knowledge so that you can use what others have found, tested or disproved to improve each and every PAY you teach. Don't be afraid to admire someone else's efforts at teaching pronunciation, but also don't be afraid to realize that what works so well for that person, group or goal isn't right for you, your students or your combined purpose in learning. In other words, the correct answer is, as always, 'It depends'.

Activity 4.5

Remembering the difference between comprehensibility and intelligibility, discuss a language learner you know (perhaps even yourself!). Can you determine what aspects influence challenges in both comprehensibility and intelligibility? If possible, record a sample of your 'subject's' spoken English (or if appropriate, any other target language) to share with the class.

Suggested Readings

Derwing, T. M. and M. J. Munro (2015) *Pronunciation Fundamentals: Evidence-based Perspectives for L2 Teaching and Research* (Amsterdam: John Benjamins Publishing).
This book has been written by two of the most important contemporary researchers in pronunciation. It is both a good introduction to the history of how pronunciation has been taught and an overview of what current research says. The book's analysis of research is clearly influenced by the authors' commitment to the importance of the intelligibility principle. Not for the beginning teacher, but excellent as an additional resource once basic ideas have been learned.

Kothalawal, C. J., T. D. Kothalawal and W. Amaratunga (2015) 'Tracing the Development of Approaches of Needs Analysis in English for Specific Purposes (ESP)', Proceedings of 8th International Research Conference, KDU. http://www.kdu.ac.lk/proceedings/irc2015/2015/msh-014.pdf.
Although this article is not specifically about pronunciation, it provides a concise overview of different types of needs analyses that are the basis for what we have called PAY in this text. The authors review eight models basically chronologically. Not an introduction to needs analysis, but an excellent review of how the term can vary depending on the needs of the analyst.

Zielinski, B. and L. Yates (2014) 'MYTH 2: Pronunciation Instruction Is Not Appropriate for Beginning-Level Learners', in L. Grant (ed.) *Pronunciation Myths: Applying Second Language Research to Classroom Teaching* (Kindle Locations 1080–82) (Ann Arbor: University of Michigan Press).
One of the best chapters in this collection of essays, this chapter refutes with research the common misconception that pronunciation instruction is best reserved for higher proficiency levels. Too often beginning students are left to their own devices in learning the sound system of the target language. This chapter shows exactly why beginning students should be given explicit pronunciation instruction.

CHAPTER 5 **Syllables and Suprasegmentals**

> Because of space constraints, this chapter gives a relatively cursory overview of tone, stress, prosody and intonation (Trofimovich and Baker, 2007). Although each of these is important and worthy of a volume on its own, one of the strengths of this series is the aim to integrate more and separate less. After examining the major views on the role of suprasegmentals in language teaching, we ask teachers to determine appropriate goals and techniques for the identifying prosodic features of speech as well as rules and practice exercises to facilitate the appropriate teaching of suprasegmentals.

Professor Chauncey Chu at the University of Florida enjoyed telling his new graduate students, 'A linguist is a person who doesn't know what a word is.' That is just the beginning of what linguists don't know. In this chapter, in addition to terms you've already learned, such as phoneme, allophone or phonotactics, we will use many terms that you already know from normal English, such as *syllable, intonation, stress, phrasing* or *rhythm*; however, we will use them in slightly different ways. Let's start with a little review of what you have learned in this text so far. We've asked you to look mainly at sounds in isolation. It's clear that we need to combine those sounds to create the elusive word and then combine them into what we can call sentences and fragments that are completely acceptable in most forms of spoken language.

We can use the term *segment* to describe the role of sounds in words. A word is made up of sound segments; that means that sounds are **segmentals**. (Well, of course, some words only have one segment: *a*.) In this way, sounds are like atoms and words are like molecules. If that chemistry metaphor is unclear or reminds you of unpleasant experiences in the lab, just ignore it. Let us give you another warning; you might want to read this chapter somewhere private, since we will ask you to read aloud all the examples. If you read them silently, you will miss most of the discussion.

Rules of Attraction: Phonotactics

Earlier we introduced the term *phonotactics* to describe the 'legal' combinations of segments to make up syllables that make up words. Native speakers and expert users of a language know subconsciously what is allowed and what isn't. For example, we know that *prst* is not a possible English word. We would really like at least one vowel in a word. On the other hand, in Czech, it means *thumb* and is a normal word that we will use again later in this chapter. Remember then that phonotactics must be viewed as language specific.

The interactions of the phonotactics of learner's native and target language can have intense influence on the pronunciation of L2 speakers. For example, ignoring some technical issues, we can say that (Mandarin) Chinese doesn't allow any consonant clusters and only allows a syllable to end in a vowel, [n], [ŋ] or an *r*-like sound. That means that most English words challenge Chinese speakers. For example, *every* word in the last sentence violated Chinese phonotactics and would require effort for the average Chinese speaker to pronounce.

The problems these interactions cause can also frustrate the instructor. When the instructor doesn't understand the phonotactics of Chinese, she is bewildered by her Chinese students who can easily pronounce *ten* but struggle to pronounce the final [t] in *net*. And both Mandarin Chinese and English speakers struggle to pronounce the traditional Cantonese form of the pronoun *I* [ŋo], as both languages only allow [ŋ] at the end of a syllable, but Cantonese has no problem with initial [ŋ].

Notice carefully, that phonotactics doesn't describe what happens to segments in a given language within the syllable or word. It describes the basic 'rules' for constructing syllables and words.

When Sounds Collide: Segments in Context

Once we've built English syllables following English phonotactics, segments (sounds) begin to interact with one another. Let's first, however, go back a bit and look at what we learned. When we discussed *phonemes*, we made it clear that we can't predict when a specific phoneme will be used. If we delete the first sound in a simple word, such as [__ æt], we can't predict which sound (segment) should fill the blank. We do know, however, that it can't be [ŋ] that can only be at the end of a syllable or [ž] unless it's a foreign word.

That first missing phoneme could be, at least, any one of the following: [b, f, g, h, k, m, n, p, r, s, t, v, č, š, ð] and each will produce a nice English word. In other words, phonemes are segmentals that change meaning.

We then looked at what happens to phonemes when they come in contact with other segmentals or positions. For example, we know that the strong *aspiration* in the English [p^h, t^h, k^h], as in *pill, till, kill* disappears completely when the same phonemes follow an [s] at the beginning of a syllable/word: *spill, still, skill*. That change is predictable and is context sensitive. We called the [p] and [p^h] *allophones* of the phoneme /p/. If we are just talking about English to 'native' speakers, we don't even need to mention the difference because it is automatic.

Of course, for many learners of English, the problem is putting the aspiration in for /p, t, k/ in initial positions because in their languages, those sounds are never aspirated and may even be a different phoneme from the aspirated form. In those cases, we need to work on helping the learners produce the difference that native speakers never even notice except as a vague notion that something isn't right when the non-native says [pɪt] instead of [pʰɪt].

Let's now take a non-English example that influences the way many speakers speak English.

Final Devoicing

In many languages, such as Dutch, German and Czech, a certain set of voiced consonants are devoiced if they are (simplifying slightly) syllable final: [b, d, t, z] become [p, t, k, s]. That is just fine in those languages, but when speakers of final **devoicing** languages speak English, they tend to apply the same process, and that can cause problems. The stereotypical 'German accent' pronunciation of English is filled with such examples: *was* [wɑz] becomes [vɑs]; and [bɛd] becomes [bɛt] (*bed* is pronounced *bet*). And if we look at the *functional load* of these contrasts, we find that it's not the general devoicing process that causes the problem, but certain specific contrasts in English. For example, the *d/t* contrast in *bed/bet* carries a 72 (from 100) functional load. Making that 'mistake' and using a [t] instead of a [d] can cause problems. On the other hand, the *b/p* contrast is only 14; that means that confusing a final *b/p*, as in *lab/lap*, is not going to cause many problems, but *d/t* will (Catford, 1987). (Do remember that although we listed what seem like very precise numbers, these examples of functional load should be seen in terms of relative rather than absolute precision.)

Sounds of a Feather: Assimilation

In all languages, there are certain seemingly universal processes that occur when segments interact. One of the most common is **assimilation**. You see the word *similar* there, we hope. Assimilation is simply making two or more sounds more similar. There are many types – backwards, forwards and others – but we look only at two related important examples in

English. Unfortunately, these examples both interact with phonotactics to create many headaches for teachers and misunderstandings for learners. Yes, we are talking about the dreaded 'correct' pronunciation of the third-person singular present tense and plural *s* suffix and the past tense suffix that we write as *–ed*. You see both in these sentences: 'He roll*ed* up the mat*s*' and 'She write*s* the word*s*'.

Say these verbs: *sob, spend, slug*. By now, you can recognize that they all end in a voiced consonant: [b, d, g]. If we want to add the *s* suffix, as in 'he sobs', we have to apply the assimilation rule. The *s* has to be voiced too. It must be pronounced [z], but we still write it as *s*: 'He sobs, she spends, it slugs', all with a fine [z] ending. Say these out loud because your eyes will try to convince your brain that the final sound is still [s].

Now, you should be able to predict what happens when we add the *–s* to verbs that end in voiceless consonants. Yes, the *s* will be pronounced [s]. But try it just to be sure. Say these verbs: *mop, bite, soak*. Remember that the *sound*, not the *spelling*, determines what happens. Yes, there is an *e* at the end of *bite*, but it's a *silent* letter, not a sound. The word ends in a [t] sound. Add *s* and you have: 'He mops, she bites and it soaks.' And as we expected, they all end with a good voiceless [s].

Whether we add the *s* as a plural marker (as in *tops, rats, oaks*) or the third person *s* (as in 'she leers, it runs, he yells'), its pronunciation must assimilate to the sound before.

The same process occurs ([z]!) with the past tense marker *–ed*. Because we are so *hyperliterate*, few untrained native speakers are aware that when we say, 'I baked cookies', the word *baked* ends in a [t] sound. Sometimes, it even takes a bit of work to convince a native speaker that that is the case. 'But, it's a *d*!' is often the answer when first asked what the final sound in *baked* is. Sometimes it's even hard to convince the native speaker that the word *baked* is only one syllable since it looks like it should have two syllables. But yes, we write *–ed* but we only say either [t] or [d]. No vowel needs to be added.

Just to be sure the process is clear, what sounds will the *–ed* have at the ends of these verbs: *slip, train* and *pay*? We hope

Activity 5.1

Put the correct symbols [s, z, t, d] for the final sound in each of these words.
1. _____ houses
2. _____ passed
3. _____ buzzed
4. _____ clocks
5. _____ rags

you said [t], [d] and [d] respectively. Now that seems easy, doesn't it? Unfortunately, although breathtakingly simple for the adult native speaker to produce, it can be difficult for the English learner and even seems to cause problems for native-speaker children as they learn to read out loud. They produce forms that they have never heard spoken by any adult native speaker of English because of the faulty way they are being taught to read, but that is another book.

Sometimes, there can be what seems to be too much assimilation, and we need to take an additional step to make sure the plural –s or the past tense marker is hearable. Take these nouns *kiss*, *rose* and *flourish* and these verbs *pat* and *need*. Try to add the plural *s* to the nouns and the past tense –*ed* to the verbs. Well, we needed to add a vowel between the word and the suffix in each case. We cannot say *kisss*. We need to insert a vowel so that we can hear the plural *s*; now we must say *kisses* with a final [z] because the vowel we inserted is *voiced*. Also note because we added a vowel, there are now two syllables. We can write *needed* just as we wrote *baked*, but now there really are *two* syllables, and the final sound really is [d], again because the vowel is voiced. This doesn't sound too difficult for anyone, but it shows what happens when we need to add a vowel. The ending must be either [z] or [d] because the vowel is voiced.

Now comes the tragic part for many learners from various languages. If the learners' L1 doesn't allow certain consonant clusters at the end of syllables, they break the consonant cluster up by – yes, you guessed it – adding a vowel. So for the learner who has a hard time saying *–kt* as in *baked*, the addition of a nice vowel between the *–k* and the *–t* solves the problem. Or it seems to. Unfortunately, we now have two problems: there should not be a vowel there, and because there is a (voiced) vowel, the *–ed* is pronounced as [d], not [t]. This is the source of the frequent mistake we hear [beˈkɪd] pronounced with two syllables.

Although assimilation is most likely a universal process, the interaction of phonotactics and assimilation can cause problems. Let's now turn to another process that, though predictable, can be problematic because of the phonotactics of learners' first language, such as was the case for the final devoicing rule.

Long and Short Vowels

The final example of the interactions of segments we look at here is quite important in improving the intelligibility of L2 learners of English. In many pedagogical textbooks written for native speakers of English, the vowel in words such as *rat* is called short, and the (first and only spoken) vowel in *rate* is called long. Those are, in fact, just labels and have nothing to do with *phonemic* or even absolute contrasts.

There are, however, languages with true phonemic contrasts between short vowels and long vowels. In those languages, long vowels always take longer to say than short vowels, and since the contrast is phonemic, we can't predict if a long or short vowel will be in the word. For example, using Czech again, the length of a vowel determines the meaning of the word. The word *pata* (*heel*, with stress on the first syllable) has two short [a] vowels, and the word *pátá* (*the fifth*, also with stress on the first syllable) has two long vowels we would represent in the IPA as [aː], where the colon means long. The vowels 'sound' the same, but the vowels in the second word literally each take twice as long to say as the vowels in the first word

(Vaughan, 2015). That is what long and short vowels are phonemically. English doesn't have that.

Just after telling you that English doesn't have phonemic long and short vowels, you can predict that we will tell you that there is some other type of long and short vowels in English. In fact, English has *two* different sources of vowel lengthening. The first type is used to display emotions. This is not predictable. Many speakers, when excited or angry (among other emotions), lengthen a key vowel as in the now clichéd 'Oh my gaaaad!' ('Oh my god!'). However, we will discuss that use of vowel lengthening later in this chapter. The other type of vowel lengthening is predictable (phonetic not phonemic!) and essential for L2 learners to understand to improve their intelligibility.

Allophonic Vowel Lengthening

Say *rib* and *rip* aloud. Say them again, but slowly. You should be able to hear that the vowel in *rib* really is longer than the vowel in *rip*. Try the same test with *bed* and *bet*. Same result? And now *pig* and *pick*. Yes, same result. (Ignore the slight difference in spelling in that example.) Finally, try it with the diphthong [aɪ] in *rise* and *rice*. Once again you can hear the difference. Did you see the pattern? When a vowel precedes a voiced consonant, such as [b, d, z], it is lengthened automatically. In other words, the difference between the diphthongs in *rise* and *rice* is allophonic. It is completely predictable (if you are a native speaker).

Working with L2 learners, it is really important to help them both hear and produce the difference, since the vowel length helps the listener know what the final consonant should be if he or she has final devoicing issues or if the speaker uses an unreleased consonant. Remembering the problems that many have with dropping final consonants or devoicing final consonants, one or two minutes of a *lightning drill* during a *teachable moment* can be very helpful. There have been many anecdotal approaches to teaching this distinction. Rubber bands and other devices have been suggested. We suggest simply asking the learners to exaggerate the differences while moving their hands from side to side as if they were painting. This technique involves the whole body as well as kinetic and visual cue. Let's look at one possible case.

During a discussion, a student says what sounds like, 'Yes, she fell and broke her rip'. Since the class has already worked on the vowel-lengthening rule before, the teacher just exclaims, 'Ah, lightning drill!' and leads the class in three repetitions of the pair *rip/rib*. While saying each, the students move one hand from side to side for the time it takes to say each word, following the teacher's lead. The teacher leads the students with the handing swiping and exaggerates the difference. The side-to-side hand swipe while saying *rib* should be three times as long as the side-to-side hand swipe while saying *rip*. Although this is really slightly longer than it would be in real speech, it follows the rule for techniques created by the first author: 'Exaggerate in class, and in real life it will be just right.' Of course, if vowel lengthening is not a problem for your PAY, don't waste the *time* to correct something that is already *right*. And we hope you noticed that the vowel in *time* is much longer than the same vowel in *right*.

Activity 5.2

Longer or shorter vowel/diphthong? Write *L* if the vowel/diphthong will be longer because of assimilation or *S* if the vowel/diphthong will be shorter because of assimilation. Remember to say the words to make sure. Don't rely on orthography.

1. _____ maze
2. _____ paste
3. _____ rain
4. _____ height
5. _____ bide

Convict the Convict: Lexical Stress

Once we have something we call words (that are made up of segmentals), then other processes can be applied to those words or chunks of words. Those processes are called *suprasegmentals*. They are 'above the sounds'. Let's look at a very traditional example involving *lexical* or *word stress*. We know that con*VICT* contrasts with *CON*vict, where the all-capital part (i.e. syllable) is stressed. The former is a verb: 'He was con*VICTED* of several crimes.' The latter is a noun: 'The *CON*vict was released early.' **Lexical stress** is applied to words, not sounds, and word stress only comes into play when there are at least two syllables.

In some languages, word stress is completely, 100 per cent predictable. Yes, once again Czech provides an example. There are no exceptions: the stress on every word with two or more syllables is on the first syllable. Well, that would make it seem easy to never make lexical stress mistakes when learning Czech. No, learners of Czech often use the stress rules of their L1 and confuse Czechs who aren't that used to hearing non-native Czech in the first place. On the other hand, the Russian language, related 'closely' to Czech, has very complex stress rules. And in a third closely related language, Polish, the stress is most often, but not always, on the next to last syllable. In other words, word stress is language specific.

Assigning word stress in English is fairly complicated and not always explainable (yet), so our discussion is rather superficial. We do have internalized rules for assigning stress to multisyllable words, but they're not perfect because we have many borrowed words or relic words that retain earlier stress patterns. Additionally, the stress rules do vary a bit from one variety of English to another. For example, in much of the United States, one hears *PO*lice [poːlis] from many and po*LICE* [pəliːs] from others. The second is considered standard, but the first is common in some areas, and you've most likely heard it on television and in films.

So what is important about lexical stress? Interactions within a word are highly dependent on lexical stress. In

English, there are usually four factors that interact in placing stress. Say *freezing*. Say it again, but exaggerate the stress on the first syllable. That syllable is (i) louder and (ii) higher in pitch. Next, and more importantly, that syllable is (iii) longer, and (iv) the vowel is fully pronounced. Now contrast that syllable with the unstressed syllable *–ing*. The unstressed syllable *–ing* is quieter, lower in pitch and shorter, and the vowel isn't pronounced as a full vowel. Contrast the pronunciation of the suffix *–ing* in *freezing* to *–ing* in the word *sing*. You can hear the difference in the vowels. We say that vowels in unstressed syllables are *reduced*. We'll mention that again when we discuss sentence stress.

Conventions for Showing Stress

Since almost everyone has access to word processing programs, we will use the following easy-to-type conventions for stress in this text. The strongest (*primary*) stress in a word will be shown with CAPS: serene becomes seRENE. If a multisyllable word has a primary and a *secondary* stress, the secondary stress will be shown with underlined lower-case letters: serendipity becomes serenDIpity. That means we have seRENE with only a primary stress, but serenDIpity with both primary and secondary stress. In many dictionaries, the two levels of stress would be marked this way: ˌseren'dipity. Did you notice the small mark before the beginning to show the first syllable carries secondary stress? No? Well, that is why we don't use that system in this book. It's not visually easy to interpret. Of course, it doesn't matter what system you use as long as you are consistent.

There are, of course, well-known differences in lexical stress between most British varieties and standard American. Ignoring the changes in vowel sounds, in the United States, we try to avoid *CONtroversy* and *haRASSment*. In British English, you can avoid *CONtroversy* as well as *conTROversy* and *HArassment* or *haRASSment*. Those small differences, however, are of no major concern as long as we ask our students to be consistent.

Something Else a Linguist Doesn't Know: The Syllable

Let's make a small detour and discuss syllables before we begin our discussion of sentence stress, also called prosody. We could write entire books (as has been done) on describing the English syllable. Let's just use a definition that is not quite 100 per cent accurate: there is one syllable for every vowel (sound). Of course, there are some problems. First, we have to remember that diphthongs are two vowels that are perceived as one: [ha^{U}s], *house*, one syllable. Next, we need to discuss certain consonants that can create a syllable on their own. As a result, we call the use of such consonants *syllabic*. Say the word *rhythm*. How many syllables are there? Two. How many vowels? Well, there is only one vowel letter; however, the last syllable sounds as if it were only an [m]; there isn't a separate vowel. Syllabic consonants are represented in the IPA by adding a vertical line under the normal consonant symbol, so the syllabic [m] is [m̩], noticing the small vertical line we have added under the second one.

Other consonants that can be syllabic are [n, l, r, m, ŋ], such as in *glutton* [glʌtn̩] and *table* [teɪbl̩]. In English, syllabic sounds are usually only in non-stressed syllables. Moreover, the syllabic sounds usually cause no real problems because even if the final syllable is pronounced as a full syllable, the 'mispronunciation' doesn't influence intelligibility. (Did you notice that *even* has a syllabic [n̩]?)

Czech (yes again!) is famous for its syllabic trilled [r] that makes written Czech look strange, as in the infamous tongue twister: *Strč prst skrz krk* that means 'Stick [your] finger through [your] throat.' Fortunately, one rarely needs to use that phrase in normal conversation.

Yes, there are few complications about the exact nature of the syllable, but those complexities are not that important in teaching English. However, it is important to teach about syllables so that both lexical and sentence stress can be improved. Using the simple, not quite accurate definition will be sufficient for most PAYs: there is one vowel sound for each syllable, and there is a syllable for each vowel sound.

Flapping: Syllables and Stress

Now that we have talked about lexical stress and the notion of the syllable, we can discuss one process that makes (mainly) American English sound different from most other varieties of World Englishes. Say, *mad, madder, bat, batter*. In most Englishes around the world, we hear [mæd, mædɚ, bæt, bætɚ]; there is a [d] in *madder* and a [t] in *batter*. However, in normal American English, we use the **flap** *d* in both *madder* and *batter* so that there is no difference in middle consonant *t/d* sounds. The symbol for that sound, which is slightly different from the normal [d], is [D]. We can say that this [D] is an allophone of both the phonemes /d/ and /t/ *intervocalically* (when it occurs between two vowels). This process produces many homonyms, such as *writer/rider* in American English. However, Americans only use the flap D when the first vowel is stressed and the second vowel isn't. In this way, stress is important also in pronunciation. We don't use the flap in *reTIRE, deTAIN,* or *ciTATION,* but we usually do in *CIting,* which sounds the same as *siding* for many speakers.

Since most Americans and many Canadians do use the flap, it is important for learners to recognize the sound, but unless their PAY involves sounding as though they were raised in Iowa, there is no need for learners to use the flap.

Follow the Bouncing Ball: Teaching Lexical Stress

There are many techniques for helping students with lexical stress. The authors prefer a very kinetic and visual technique. We call it *conducting class*. When practising the stress of words, the instructor is an *orchestra conductor,* and the students are conductor trainees. The instructor uses the hand as the baton and 'draws' the stress, pitch and length of each syllable in an exaggerated manner in the air. By having the students (who may be very resistant to using their hands at first) imitate the exaggerated motions of the teacher's hand as visual and kinetic cues, the pitch and length of the syllable are almost automatically 'pulled along'. There are examples of this technique on the *SeeItSayIt English*™ website (www.seeenglishsounds.com). Of course, instructors must be very careful about the *A* in PAY. There are audiences that would consider the technique juvenile. Only *you* can decide if it is appropriate.

Was that Thirteen or Thirty?

Using the conducting technique we just discussed and our discussion of lexical stress, we can now address a common problem of intelligibility: numbers above twelve that involve both stress and flapped *D*s in most American varieties.

How many times have we asked a student, 'Did you mean fifty or fifteen?' If we use contrastive stress with the *SeeItSayIt English*™ conducting techniques, we can have lightning drills that will help students hear and produce the difference.

Once you have practised the conducting drill technique, you can use it for the very quick lightning drills that keep the students interested about as long as they can be. Again, the quick two-minute drill is more effective when done at the right teachable moment rather than being an hour of disengaged repetition. Depending on your PAY, you may find other pairs that might need to be visually contrasted. The other standard one is the verb/noun contrast in *conVICT/CONvict*, *reCORD/REcord* or *proDUCE/PROduce*. But you will find many on your own as you start looking for them. Now instead of just asking, 'Did you mean fifteen or fifteen?', you can use the conducting signs for them as you ask, and hopefully your students will be able to self-correct.

Activity 5.3 Conducting Class

1. First try it yourself. Yes, raise your hands, and while you conduct, say *thirty* as THIRdy [*sic* – with a flapped *D*, not a *t*] in your best American accent. The hand starts high, just above eyelevel, lingers there while you say *THIR* and then drops quickly to throat level as you slightly exaggerate the shortness of *dy*. Now of course, if you really do always and without exception say *THIRty* with a [t] rather than [D], please continue doing so. However, if your normal pronunciation involves the flapped *D*, use it. It's one more clue for the students to be able to recognize *thirty*. Now do the reverse for *thirTEEN*, again exaggerating slightly the shortness of *thir* and the length of *TEEN* with strong aspiration on the [t]. Begin at throat level with your conducting hand, and then quickly raise your hand to eye level, and keep it there as you move it to the side.
2. Now work in pairs, taking turns being the teacher and the student.
   a. Using any of the confusing pairs from *thirteen/thirty* through *nineteen/ninety*, the teacher can tell the student: '*Show* me xx!' And the students use only their hands, no sounds.
   b. The teacher now does the reverse, 'conducting' the number silently only with the hand. First show a number with your fingers, such as four, and then 'conduct' either fourteen or forty. The student tells you which one you signed.

Speaking of Americans: Global Features

Before we turn to how stress and intonation influence sentences, let's talk about something few pronunciation texts talk about: global features. Linda Grant (2014) adds *volume*, *speed* (words per minute) and *articulatory setting* to the more traditional suprasegmentals. The first two are rather obvious, and we all know anecdotally that the stereotypical female Japanese student can barely be heard while it's easy to find the Americans (and several other groups!) by just following the loud conversations in a public place.

Speed can be a problem for learners, both as speakers and listeners. In training future ELT teachers, the authors have their trainees post the single word *SLOW* in large letters on a sheet of paper they hang on the back wall of the practice room. Even though each of the letters can be used to mean other features (such as standard, loud and even 'whatever works' for the letter *w*) as the course progresses, the first meaning is essential for most new teachers: Slow down. Oddly, the same is also necessary for some non-native speakers who rush through their conversations. Slow down and speak up. Now thinking of your native language community, whether it is English or something else, there are most likely particular groups that are stereotypically notorious for speaking too fast (i.e. New Yorkers) or too slow (in the United States, people from Mississippi), although this is often impressionistic rather than absolute (Roach, 1998). A characteristic speed or tempo is part of each language and even dialects.

The final feature, Grant's *articulatory setting*, also called *voice-setting features*, should be explored and exploited much more frequently in teaching pronunciation than it is today. Let's take a non-speech example first. It's often easy for keen observers to figure out where strangers are from simply by their posture and their gait. We can see that the Chinese teacher from Beijing does not hold himself or walk the way the Chinese-American teacher from the Mississippi Delta does. There is muscle memory created by 'walking Chinese' or 'walking Canadian' for many years. The same can be said for certain athletes. We are always surprised when someone is a superstar in two or more professional sports because it's hard to change the way the muscles react, after years of intensive practice in one sport, to the reactions needed for another sport. In that way, speech is exactly the same. Years of speaking

Mexican Spanish or Standard Thai creates a basic setting for all the parts of speech process. Go online and play a few YouTube videos from different languages, but with the volume off. You will be able to see the subtle differences. Look at the lips and the tension in the jaw, and try to imitate that position.

The first author uses *articulatory setting* in teaching both English and German. In what might seem offensive to some, he asks the student to speak their native language while imitating the accent of the target language. So, the English speaker tries to put on a German accent in English while the Arabic speaker speaks Arabic with an American accent. Then the class tries to describe the different ways the muscles, jaws, tongue and lips worked together. Later when a lightning *drill* might be useful, the instructors says, 'English (German, Arabic, etc.) mouth', and the students try to set their mouths appropriately. This might be thought of as a *role play* for the mouth.

Once we have thought about the global features of volume, tempo or speed, and articulatory setting, we can finally turn to the sentence.

Stringing the Words Along: Sentence Stress

The basic purpose of *non-predictable* stress in English sentences is to make clear what is important (usually new) information

Activity 5.4

'Know thyself' was a famous aphorism used by many Greek philosophers and one that is part of our PAY. Could you use the 'speak like an Englishman in our language' technique we've just discussed? Why or why not? Would you be able to use it with the different audiences (the *A* in PAY) that you might encounter? Remember: what worked for the authors of this text may not work for you, and vice versa.

and what isn't that important (usually old) information. Of course, stress is just one of several ways to highlight new and old information or to make clear what is important and what isn't. When we do use stress to contrast old and new, we call it *contrastive stress*. To show how this stress works, we almost always need to use dialogues, since a contrast requires something with which something else can be contrasted.

1. Two women, Adele and Berta, looking at a book and drinking coffee:
   Adele: *Did FRED give you that book?* [Fred is stressed because he is the new information; book is the old.]
   Berta: *No, JUDY did.* [Judy is stressed because she is new information.]

2. Two women, Adele and Berta, looking at a book and drinking coffee:
   Adele: *WHAT did Fred give you for your birthday?*
   Berta: *Ha. He FORGOT my birthday.* [Forgot is unexpected, new information.]

3. Two women, Adele and Berta, looking at a book and drinking coffee:
   Adele: *You aren't drinking your coffee. Would you like some TEA instead?* [Coffee is old and tea is new and therefore stressed.]
   Berta: *No, but do you have any hot CHOCOLATE?*

Please don't try to teach contrastive stress in isolation. It has to be in context. There are horrible exercises that ask students to change the stress in one sentence repeatedly. Don't do it!
   Example of bad exercise:

1. Abdullah DROVE to Boston yesterday.
2. Abdullah drove to BOSTON yesterday.
3. Abdullah drove to Boston YESTERDAY.
4. ABDULLAH drove to Boston yesterday.

Unless the students are given the contexts in which these different responses could be used, this exercise is a waste of time for *beginning* students. It could be modified for *advanced* students by asking them which question each variant would answer. Students could match the questions below with the correct version, but again you have to decide whether this works for your students.

In most cases, a *wh-* question asks for new information, so the piece of information that is requested (who, what, where, when) would be the new information and therefore would be the stressed word.

A. WHAT did Abdullah do yesterday?
   He DROVE to Boston yesterday.
   [Abdullah is now old information and can be replaced by a pronoun.]

B. WHERE did Abdullah drive yesterday?
   He drove to BOSTON.
   [Yesterday is now old information and can be deleted.]

C. WHEN did Abdullah drive to Boston?
   He drove there YESTERDAY.
   [Since to Boston is now old information, we replace it with there.]

D. WHERE did Abdullah drive yesterday?
   He drove to BOSTON.
   [Yesterday is now old information and can be deleted.]

E. WHO drove to Boston yesterday?
   ABDULLAH did. (or even just ABDULLAH)
   [Since everything else is old information, we can just delete it.]

If you were also reviewing question formation, you could give the answer and ask the students to generate the correctly stressed question, and that would ensure that pronunciation was integrated into the lesson.

The take-away from sentence intonation is that sentence stress is often important in terms of sharing information; if you remember that fact, you will understand that teaching intonation is more communicatively based and is not just about repeating sentence models.

We mentioned earlier that not all languages use contrastive stress to identify old and new information. It's not part of Czech, which uses word order instead and rarely varies sentential stress. As a result, Czechs and many other speakers need to practise exaggerating the stressed component of sentences so that the stress levels will be normal in normal conversation. *Exaggerate* now to get it right later.

Resolving or Avoiding Ambiguity

In an attempt to save space, newspapers often accidentally produce ambiguous headlines. For example, let's look at a recent headline in the popular newspaper *USA Today* about the 2016 American presidential primaries going on while this book was being written.

The headline was 'Trump attacks fly fast at debate' (Jackson and Jacobs, 2016). Only the proper *spoken stress* can tell us if Mr Trump was attempting the fabled 'grab a fly with chopsticks' stunt of so many bad Kung Fu movies; if his opponents were attacking him; or if Mr Trump was attacking his opponents. In speech that would be clear. Of course, there are other syntactic devices that would allow us to make explicit which of those meanings was meant. 'It was a fly that Mr Trump attacked at the debate.' For example, to make sure our audience knows our stance, we often use stressed *sentential adverbs* as instructions for decoding our message. Contrast

Activity 5.5

Create an exercise to show how contrastive stress is used to answer the *wh-* questions in English along the lines of 'Abdullah drove to Boston yesterday'. In pairs, make sure your colleagues can answer your prompts correctly. For example, 'Brent cooked SHRIMP yesterday' should elicit 'What did Brent cook yesterday?'

'*Fortunately*, he was fired' with '*Unfortunately*, he was fired.' That happy/sad distinction would be easy in speech, even without the sentential adverbs. However, in this world filled with text messages (short message service, or SMS, in most of the world), laconic e-mails or Twitter, the written word often leads to misunderstanding. We've even created emoticons to help. ;-)

And do remember that not all languages allow the use of stress to indicate importance. Some use word order, special particles or structures such as 'No, not Fred. It was Jane, who discovered it.' In English, we could just say, 'Not Fred, JANE.' That means that we have to help our students understand, recognize and produce meaningful stress to manage information.

Stressful English: Stress and Syllable-timed Language

There is, however, also a basic, more predictable *rhythm* to English that is the result of word stress embedded into sentences. English is called a **stress-timed language**, in contrast to Japanese and French, which are called **syllable-timed languages**. We will avoid any theoretical arguments about the correctness of that statement because the division is considered controversial by some. Nonetheless, the concepts work well as heuristics.

As we noted before, in English, which is *stress-timed*, stressed syllables are louder, higher in pitch and *longer* than unstressed syllables. Also, the vowels in stressed syllables are *full*. Remember the two pronunciations of *police* in American English. If the first syllable is pronounced (not the standard version), the *o* is pronounced [po:lis] louder, higher in pitch and longer. However, that same vowel is reduced to a *schwa* [ə] that is shorter, quieter and lower in pitch when the second syllable is stressed: [pəli:s] in the standard form.

In *syllable-timed* languages, each syllable is basically the same length whether it is stressed or unstressed. And importantly, unstressed vowels are not reduced. The vowel stays the same. Try that with the English word *police*. Say [poːliːs]. It sounds almost mechanical.

This constant contrast between loud, higher pitched, long, clear syllables and short, quiet, lower pitched, reduced syllables gives English its characteristic *rhythm*. It is probably no accident that Shakespeare and many other poets chose the well-known poetic foot *iambic pentameter* for much of their work; it sounds just about like normal spoken English. However, the traditional literary method of just marking the stress used in literature ignores the change in pitch and length that is an essential part of English lexical stress; of course, since the convention of just marking stress was meant for native speakers of English, there was no reason to mark the other changes because they are predictable ... for native speakers. Look at this example from Shakespeare in which the / symbol represents a stressed syllable and x an unstressed one. It doesn't show that the / syllable is longer or higher in pitch. You now know that more is going on than just a making the stressed syllable louder.

x / x / x / x / x /
But *soft*, what *light* through *yon*der *win*dow *breaks*?
(*Romeo and Juliet*)

The necessity to stress pitch, volume and length is also one of the reasons that the traditional 'pencil-tapping' approach to teaching English stress is neither complete nor completely effective.

If you are a native speaker of English who has never thought about what English sounds like to others, you might want to watch the YouTube® video of a 1972 Italian hit song 'Prisencolingensinanciusol' [*sic*] that is written in 'gibberish'. It was a parody of the way English sounds to Italians. Listening to that parody, you get a sense of what others hear. Likewise, if you speak French, you might be familiar with the opposite, a collection of 'French' poems that are in fact English nursery rhymes spoken in a truly stereotypical French accent, *Mots d'heures, gousses, rames* [i.e. Mother Goose rhymes] (Van Rooten, 1980). Both of these examples remind us that there is a prototypical rhythm to each language. And these rhythms influence learners' accents as they learn new languages.

Melting Syllables: Connected Speech

You have read now several times that unstressed syllables are reduced. In fact, in normal speech many of these syllables and indeed short words are so reduced that they merge into other syllables or words. Most of us who have taught first-year university composition to native speakers have seen the following in the rough draft of an essay: 'She *should of* [sic] pushed him overboard. But she was so *usta* [sic] just ignoring him.' Yes, that is what some native speakers write for *should have* and *used to* when they're not careful.

It has always been traditional that we teach special lessons about the reduced forms for words such as *to* that becomes either [tə] or [də]. For example, we would pull two sentences out of context and teach 'I *hope to* leave tomorrow' [hoptə] and 'I *need to* leave tomorrow' [ni:də] to show what happens after voiceless and voiced sounds. (Now there is a pattern that seems familiar, isn't it?) Of course, that approach is ironic, as in isolation they're not reduced. We think it would be more appropriate to do a quick *lightning drill* when it is useful. This is especially true since so many learners of English now hear so much 'authentic' English in movies and in songs, that we sometimes have the opposite problem. We need to remind texting-fluent students not to use *gonna, wanna* or *shoulda* in writing. If we emphasize and exaggerate the difference between stressed and unstressed syllables both at the word and sentence level, the reduced forms normally take care of themselves, but do not hesitate to bring the process to learners' attention explicitly and briefly when necessary. Yes, it depends on the PAY.

One exception to the 'don't bother about fixing it' rule is for very visual students. Some visual students seem to be reading the texts of their spoken conversation word by word from what seems to be a written text in their mind. Especially, if they also come from syllable-timed languages, their resulting speech sounds very artificial. Again exaggerated lightning drills with 'shouting/lengthening and whispering/shortening' stressed and unstressed syllables bring attention to the problem.

Learners' lack of reduced forms in English or their use in other languages, coupled with the other language's basic rhythm, can also create attitudinal problems. We mentioned earlier that Czech is without exception always stressed on the first syllable of each word. Additionally, non-stressed syllables are not reduced. As a result, it is possible to have a (very) long unstressed vowel in Czech. Professor J. Volín (whose name does indeed have a long unstressed [i:]) at Charles University's Institute of Phonetics agreed informally that the intonation patterns that might be used naturally by Americans speaking Czech often lead to the impression that the American speakers are not sincere or are pretending something (Vaughan, 2015). On the other hand, as Vaughan also points out, most speakers of English think that when Czechs speak English, they sound bored, disinterested and monotonous because there seems to be no distinction between stressed and unstressed syllables in pitch, volume and, importantly, length; it is just monotonous (2015). Think now about the stereotypical 'emotional' state of non-native speakers, and you can see that our perceptions are in reality a function not of emotions, but of different stress patterns and the resulting interactions or lack of interactions with other sounds in the words and sentences.

When necessary, a few lightning drills with reduced forms (e.g. 'He shoulda gone. She hasta help him. You wanna see a movie?') will bring more success in the long run than hours of describing what happens. Yes, helping students exaggerate the difference in pitch, length and loudness by using your hands and making them use theirs can help resolve these problems, but again, they almost never influence intelligibility except in extreme 'computer speech' cases. Again the PAY is what you should consider.

Roller coasters: Sentence Intonation

We have discussed lexical, contrastive stress and basic rhythm in English, but we haven't said much about the different *intonation contours* that are usually part of pronunciation texts. In many texts, there are pages of musical notation to show pitch or numbers that represent abstract pitch levels. However, for the most part, they are not useful for the beginner, and the advanced students have already 'mastered' the basic sentence patterns. The magic word here is *pattern*. Yes, we will go back to the 1960s and employ the ALM backwards build-up and choral response, but in a more focused fashion.

Since few teachers have received sufficient pronunciation training, they often repeat half-truths and other legends of the classroom. How many times have you heard a teacher say, 'In English, the voice rises in pitch at the end of a question.' Well, no, that's not really true. It's more complex than that, but just as it was intentionally ignored in ALM, we don't need to spell it out. Rather, as Professor Judy Gilbert (2008) suggests, let the students hear the pattern or, using the new word for pattern, template, (sample yes/no questions, *wh-* questions, commands, statements, etc.) several times to internalize the rhythm. After they've heard the template a few times, the students can try it. Now using the 'conducting class' technique mentioned earlier, the instructor can lead the class in delightful choral responses. The air should be full of moving hands, heads and mouths. Both authors have worked in Chinese environments in which choral response was an active, exciting part of the classroom. Of course, since some of the classes had up to eighty students, choral response there was a logical answer to logistics too. However, these choral activities must be *lightning drills* that never last over two or three minutes. Otherwise, boredom ensues. Using the conducting class, the instructor demonstrates kinetically, visually and orally the basic intonation patterns without complex charts that look more like pieces of twentieth-century atonal music than English. As with all the lightning drills, when intense attention is devoted to the activity, we have more success from literally seconds of such drills than from hours of unfocused, seemingly meaningless explanations and worksheets. Again, notice that we are giving you anecdotal evidence, not traditional 'quantitative' research.

Conclusion

Pronunciation instruction is essential to most learning contexts. But unless you are training spies or movie stars, it is rarely appropriate to promise or even try for near-native pronunciation. Especially in the new world of English as a Lingua Franca, native pronunciation is almost an oxymoron since there are many more non-natives than natives.

We also need to consider the PAY before we start any instruction, since that determines so much, including which variety of English to hold up as a pedagogical model. For example, if you were a Texan working in Texas, it would make no sense to teach New Zealand English that tends not to reduce unstressed vowels, unlike most of the other varieties of English (Bauer, 2015). Of course, the opposite would be just as true if you were a New Zealander working in New Zealand.

Once we have established an appropriate PAY, we can help students understand the 'mouth setting' (articulatory setting) that plays the role in speech that the basic 'athletic stance' plays in most sports. From there we can produce oral templates to help learners internalize these patterns. With lightning drills, conducting classes and many other appropriate techniques that work for your PAY, we can increase intelligibility and comprehensibility, the goal for almost all modern language teaching and learning.

Suggested Readings

Gilbert, J. B. (2008) *Teaching Pronunciation: Using the Prosody Pyramid* (New York: Cambridge University Press).

https://www.tesol.org/docs/default-source/new-resource-library/teaching-pronunciation-using-the-prosody-pyramid.pdf?sfvrsn=0
An important resource booklet available for free from TESOL International and written by one of the leaders in pronunciation teaching. In fifty-six pages, Professor Gilbert uses simple line drawings and many visuals to help teachers understand the importance of the suprasegmentals in producing 'clear speech'. Her explanation of each level of the prosody pyramid makes the topic very accessible. Written for the practitioner, this should be read by every teacher interested in helping students speak more effectively.

Stop Saying: Double Contractions.
http://www.bbc.co.uk/learningenglish/english/course/upper-intermediate/unit-1/session-4
The first in an online series of focused lessons on specific common problems for most learners of English, this exercise is an excellent example of how making speech 'less clear' by using reduced forms, such as contractions, actually makes speech much more authentic and thereby clearer. Compare a very computer-like pronunciation of 'I would have ...' to the much more natural (and neutral) so-called double contraction 'I'd've'. The lesson could serve as a model for other issues your students might have.

CHAPTER 6

Language Varieties & English as a Lingua Franca

The emergence of English as a Lingua Franca (ELF) has led to a shared ownership of the varieties of English by both native (NS) and non-native speakers (NNS). This chapter discusses the topic of ELF as it relates to the teaching and learning of pronunciation in ESL and EFL contexts, and it develops the conversation further to examine the role of language varieties in the teaching of second and foreign languages. We refer to the recent work that has been done on accent and identity, but ask the teachers to determine their own stance on the issues. Special emphasis is given to the role of non-native teachers in the teaching of pronunciation.

With 'the total number of English speakers globally ... between 500 million and 1 billion' or more, there is no doubt about the importance of English in the twenty-first century (Brutt-Griffler, 2006, p. 690). English is currently spoken as a native language, as a second language, as a foreign language, as a Lingua Franca and as an international language. Though French may still claim to be a de jure international language of diplomacy, English is the de facto working language of diplomacy and business for much of the world. Even in 2003, David Crystal (2003) noted that NNSs of English then outnumbered NSs by a ratio of 3 to 1, and David Graddol (2003) offers that the percentage of NSs will only continue to decline in the coming decades. This shift in the demographics of English language speakers is having a dramatic effect on the way the language is perceived, taught and learned. English is currently being spoken or learned by more people in more contexts than any other language now or ever in the past; however, it is not just the number of speakers that gives English its status and prestige. McKay (2002) states that one of the defining characteristics of a global language that makes English so important is the fact that it is 'no longer linked to a single culture or nation but serves both global and local needs as a language of wider communication' (p. 24). However, it could be argued that at almost no point in its history has English truly belonged to a single culture, but rather has been a product of language contact and movement just like other languages. Just try telling a Scotts(wo)man that Scottish and English culture are the same. Just as English has evolved from Proto-Indo-European to Proto-Germanic, and from Anglo-Saxon or Old English into Middle English and eventually into Modern English, it is continuing to adapt and develop to the different contexts where it is being spoken. Recognizing this, teachers of English(es) are put in the position of helping their students become a part of a larger global community rather than simply integrating into a single culture. In this way, we are not adding a Culture 2 to our students' Culture 1, but instead we are giving them a *skeleton key* (a key that can open most locks) to exploring almost all cultures. This distinction will be important as we consider exactly with whom students of the English language are preparing to communicate.

When discussing the teaching of pronunciation, issues arise concerning the variety and selection of target phonemes to be taught. Some accents and dialects may bestow prestige upon their speakers; such has been the case with speakers of Standard

Activity 6.1

Do you agree with the assertion that English has become a world language that no longer belongs to 'native' speakers of English? Why or why not?

American English, who may benefit from the impression that they are educated (Rahman, 2008). Other dialects often face intense discrimination, as has historically been the case with African-American Vernacular English (AAVE), also called Black American English (BAE), which is still frequently regarded as ungrammatical or inferior in spite of the brilliant work by scholars such as Labov (1966) to prove its validity as a complete variety of English. Interestingly enough, like its speakers, AAVE has been a dialect that has been both criticized and marginalized while also being commodified and marketed to the world through popular culture. Now, it is also obvious in this case that it is not the dialect that causes discrimination, but rather it is a product of the racism African Americans have continued to suffer throughout the history of the United States.

Other accents and dialects might indicate membership in a specific social group, thus granting access and opportunity to their speakers. This can be seen in diglossic situations where one model of language or dialect can be reserved for home, family and community while the other is primarily used with the 'other' in 'higher' contexts. There are standard examples of this in Norway and Haiti. Pronunciation and dialect can be tied to different identities, such as race, class, region, social group and even sexual orientation, and the social power dynamics inherent in those distinctions, so teaching or learning a specific variety can mean the acceptance of one group or rejection of another.

When teaching a language such as German, which is only spoken in a few countries and has clearly identifiable norms, identifying the distinctions to teach is relatively simple, although the basic PAY must still be clarified. For example, no

Activity 6.2

Ask your students which speakers have the 'best' accent in English and which have the 'worst'. What reasons do they come up with for the distinction?

Activity 6.3

1. Compare the variety of English heard on different international news channels that you might know such as the BBC, CNN, China Central Television (CCTV), Deutsche Welle, and so on.
2. What aspects of the pronunciation make it difficult to understand?
3. What aspects make it easy to understand?
4. How do you see English varying among the channels?

one teaches any of the varieties of Swiss German outside Switzerland unless there is a specific reason to learn a specific variety. On the other hand, even the simplest decision on which form of 'How are you?' to teach becomes more complicated when considering dialects of French or regional varieties of Arabic or Chinese, although certain varieties are generally preferred for the language classroom. Of course, the instruction of English is somewhat complicated by the colonial history of the United Kingdom, which ensured that while the sun now sets on the British Empire, the sun never sets on the English language. Over fifty years ago, the British Linguist John Rupert Firth discussed the complicated nature of classifying Englishes, commenting that:

> English is an international language in the Commonwealth, the Colonies and in America. International in the sense that English serves the American way of life and might be called American, it serves the Indian way of life and has recently been declared an Indian language within the framework of the federal constitution. In another sense, it is international not only in Europe but in Asia and Africa, and serves various African ways of life and is increasingly the all-Asian language of politics. Secondly, and I say 'secondly' advisedly, English is the key to what is described in a common cliché 'the British way of life'. (1956, p. 97, as cited in Kachru (2006, p. 363))

What Firth noted is being realized today as teachers around the world work to find an *appropriate* model of English pronunciation to teach their students. Normally, ESL teachers in the United Kingdom, the United States, Australia, Canada or New Zealand will by default teach their regional variety. The choice becomes less obvious elsewhere, although the South African teaching in Nebraska will still teach, if indirectly through modelling alone, South African English. In fact, the choice is not only difficult for teachers, but it can be a difficult decision for students as well. Grammar teachers, junior linguists and language mavens the world over are likely to embrace certain dialects as more or less correct or prestigious. As a result, students are often left questioning which variety of spoken English they should be learning. Non-native teachers may question which model of English they should be teaching. Regardless of the fact that these questions are undoubtedly charged with underlying socio-political meanings and implications, these questions are in fact 'non-questions' since the answer is unequivocal: it depends on what is appropriate in the given context, who is being taught and who is teaching. Yes, we are back to PAY. If it has been unclear before this point, it should be obvious that both authors subscribe to the principles of **descriptive linguistics** and prefer, when appropriate, Communicative Language Teaching (CLT) that focuses more on naturally occurring language and appropriateness in context than prescribing specific norms. Nonetheless, in pedagogical terms, we must inform students about the sociolinguistic implications of their choices, such as using *me and X* as subjects in sentences such as '*Me and Max* will come back later.' This form is perceived in the United States at least as uneducated and 'low class', and must never be used in formal writing, although learners of English will often hear such forms in informal 'non-standard' English.

As a result, we teach with the belief that different learners will need different models, which will be defined by the situation in which English is being spoken – yes, PAY.

Activity 6.4

1. Take an example of a cartoon with characters who speak English with different accents (e.g. *Dora the Explorer*, *The Simpsons*, *Loony Toons*, any Disney movie, etc.) and analyse how different accents are matched to the character who speaks them.
2. Take Jar Jar Binks from the *Star Wars* Episodes I–III (https://www.youtube.com/watch?v=_FLhO7ZnKHs) and do the same.
3. Look at YouTube® for 'Sophisticated Trump' (https://www.youtube.com/watch?v=qUGT3ogGtiI), a *Fox News* interview of Donald Trump that has been dubbed into Received Pronunciation, and do the same.

Since English serves as a global Lingua Franca, teachers are realizing that ownership of the language no longer belongs (or possibly never belonged) to only those speakers from what Kachru (1985) in a now very outdated model identified as Inner Circle countries, those countries like the United Kingdom, the United States, Canada, Australia and New Zealand, where English was traditionally spoken as a native language and the norms for the language are or were set. Ownership of the language is also now recognized as belonging to speakers from Kachru's so-called Outer Circle countries, like India, Singapore and the Philippines, that were colonized by Inner Circle countries. And now, in what Kachru called the Expanding Circle, countries such as China and Saudi Arabia, English is almost essential to being educated or for operating in the global market. It seems the circle has already expanded.

With the growing realization that English could not be treated as a monolith, and that even within these contexts, there was considerable variation in the norms of English, the concept of World Englishes emerged in the 1960s; it became a field of study by 1978 with the emergences of the International Association for World Englishes. As NS and NNS of English use the language in different contexts, ownership of the global language is shared, and both can lay claim to equally 'correct' models of the language. Graddol (2007) expands the argument further, stating, 'Native-speaker norms are becoming less relevant as English becomes a component of basic education in many countries' (p. 14). In this changing climate, standards and patterns of English are evolving in each context, and these will hold far more relevance to local speakers than a foreign model of Received Pronunciation (RP) or Standard American English (SAE).

The teaching and learning of pronunciation in ESL and EFL contexts was influenced by the communicative language teaching (CLT) revolution of the 1970s and 1980s, which encouraged a focus on intelligibility and comprehensibility in ELT. Before that there was often a curriculum-imposed, intrinsic motivation about sounding native-like that placed target native accents as an ideal, since communicating with NS and learning their culture was seen to be the goal of language instruction. Even native speakers of non-prestige accents were often not allowed to teach pronunciation. It was this ideal that has led to the 'native speaker bias' in both textbooks and teacher training materials, as noted by Jenkins (2000), and a very imperialist native-speakerism: 'The ideology behind the privileged status of native speakers as language teachers, particularly affects teachers working in the private sector, where the myth of the superiority of the native speaker is used as bait for paying students' (Petrić, 2009, p. 141). Yes, even today, many job ads demand that the applicants be 'native speakers', and that credential is more important than training and experience in many positions. What is not often explicitly stated is that applicants must be native speakers of only a few prestige accents found in the inner circle of the Inner Circle. Additionally, the imperialistic, native speaker bias can be harmful to students of the English language who may disregard the variety of English they or their neighbours happen to speak;

furthermore, it can be especially demoralizing to those students who are learning at a point in their lives where so-called perfect pronunciation is especially difficult to obtain. Because we know that non-native speakers outnumber native speakers, English is spoken in more contexts than in just the so-called Inner Circle countries, and there exist numerous models of 'native' English; the field is evolving past its outdated models, but the real world lags far behind.

To deal with the changing climate of ELT and the understanding of English as it is being used globally, Jenkins focused attention on the core features of pronunciation that ensured intelligibility in English. Do remember that there are critics of her work who maintain that her work is still too anecdotal and not quantitative enough. Nonetheless, it is a very good start.

After researching miscommunication data, Jenkins proposed the **Lingua Franca Core** (LFC) in her book *The Phonology of English as an International Language* in 2000. The LFC identified the features of pronunciation most essential to effective communication in English. As you look at parts of her work list here (Table 6.1), do remember that RP stands for (British) Received Pronunciation, which some also call 'BCC English' or even the more culturally bound 'Oxford English'. GA is General American, which we have been calling SAE (Standard American English). Also remember that rhotic means an *r*-sound. Most American accents are 'rhotic'; there is an [ɹ] that can be heard in both *heard* and *car*. Many British and most 'English' (i.e. from England!) accents are non-rhotic; not an /r/ to be heard in *heard* or *car*. As an aside and comment on how quickly 'things' can change, it should be noted that the non-rhotic characteristic of British English is actually recent and wasn't really universal in RP until the beginning of the nineteenth century. Yes, remember Shakespeare said [hiːɹ] not [hiə].

With its heavy focus on segmentals, the LFC differs from well-established pronunciation texts such as Judy Gilbert's (1984) *Clear Speech* or Celce-Murcia, Brinton and Goodwin's *Teaching Pronunciation: A Reference for Teachers of English to Speakers of Other Languages* (1996), both of which place far

Table 6.1 EFL and ELF pronunciation targets

	EFL Target Traditional Syllabus	ELF Target Lingua Franca Core
1. The consonantal inventory	all sounds close RP/GA RP non-rhotic /r/ GA rhotic /r/ RP intervocalic [t] GA intervocalic [ɾ]	all sounds except /θ/, /ð/ but approximations of all others acceptable rhotic /r/ only intervocalic /t/ only
2. Phonetic requirements	rarely specified	aspiration after /p/,/t/,/k/ appropriate vowel length before voiced/voiceless consonants
3. Consonant clusters	all word positions	word initially, word medially
4. Vowel quality	long-short contrast	long-short contrast
5. Main stress	important	critical

EFL and ELF pronunciation targets: core features Jenkins (2002, p. 99) as cited in Jenkins (2007, p. 23).

more emphasis on suprasegmentals for learners' attainment of fluency. Jenkins' approach can be seen as a remedy to native speaker bias in ELT, as non-native teachers (NNESTs) can provide students with a pronunciation model that makes use of all the essential features of the LFC essential to intelligibility. Within the context of ELF, it is the individual consonant and vowel sounds that *might* most readily help communication, allowing speakers to clarify, while the reduced sounds that taught in suprasegmental training might lead to miscommunication between NNSs.

Currently, even the nature of intelligibility is being debated in the context of English as a Lingua Franca (ELF), English as an International Language (EIL) and World Englishes. ELF and EIL may at times be considered to be synonymous, but there is a clear distinction between the two. As a *Lingua Franca* is traditionally understood to be a common 'non-native' language that is used between speakers of different languages, *English as a Lingua Franca* is usually considered to be the case where L2 speakers are speaking English with each other. In other words, it is the English used by the Cambodian tour guide speaking to the French tourist. Not an English or American person in sight.

ELF is used internationally, in each of Kachru's circles, in academic conferences and journals, in aviation communication between air-traffic control towers and pilots, in business contexts. On the other hand, EIL encapsulates both those cases where L1 and L2 English speakers are present, and in this context different varieties of English are recognized as belonging to their speakers' identities.

Given the different contexts in which ELF and EIL are used, NS norms will not necessarily be required for different English speakers to communicate. Questioning whether (universal) intelligibility is always a goal for an English language learner, Kachru and Smith (2008) posit that it's not 'necessary for every user of English to be intelligible, at all times, to every other user of English. One's English needs to be intelligible only to those with whom (s)he is attempting to communicate' (p. 60). For example, when delegates from member states of the Association of Southeast Asian Nations (ASEAN), a political and economic organization made up of ten Southeast Asian countries, meet, they speak in English, as that is the organization's official working language, and an 'Inner Circle' NS's understanding of

Activity 6.5

1. Which English variety or varieties are preferred in your teaching context? Why?
2. Do your students prefer the same variety/ies that their instructors do?
3. How are preferences changing/not changing?

the meeting would be irrelevant to their business. The norms and standards of the appropriate form of English will be easily recognizable to Southeast Asians. Additionally, in EIL settings such as this, speakers who maintain L1 language markers may be deliberately asserting their identity in their L2. It could be argued that NSs of English can be at a disadvantage in EIL situations, especially if the NSs speak in a regional jargon or with pronunciation patterns that are not common for the context.

This understanding of the different contexts of English, and the shared ownership it has in an international context, changes the dynamic for English teachers who might have been trained in a binary conception of ESL and EFL, or as it seems to many NS speakers in their home countries, 'here' and 'there'. Relating those core features of spoken language that inhibit communication in EIL contexts to the non-core features that do not inhibit communication, Seidlhofer (2005) suggests that teachers focus more on

> general language awareness and communication strategies; these may have more 'mileage' for learners than striving for mastery of fine nuances of native speaker language use that are communicatively redundant or even counter-productive in lingua franca settings, and which may anyway not be teachable in advance, but only learnable by subsequent experience of the language (p. 340).

Not all scholars are convinced that teaching pronunciation only for communication and intelligibility will be sufficient to meet English language learners' needs. The simple answer is, of course, of course not! Nothing is likely to meet the needs of all PAYs.

The assertions of Jenkins, Seidlhofer and others that teaching ELF allows for diversions from NS norms have not gone without criticism from both NS and NNS researchers. Kuo (2006) contends that teaching in the ELF context should still focus on NS norms in order to 'ease or smooth the flow of conversation, to reduce the listener's burden of processing information and to satisfy learners' needs that stretch beyond merely international intelligibility' (2006, p. 220). Graddol agrees, asserting, 'The use of English as a global lingua franca requires intelligibility and the setting and maintaining of standards', while also admitting that 'the increasing adoption of English as a second language, where it takes on local forms, is leading to fragmentation and diversity' (p. 3). More important than the view of researchers on either side of the debate, or even of NESTs and NNESTs, are the perspective and desires of English language students, most of whom have an idealized accent in mind. The authors are often asked by expert users of English around the world, 'Do I sound American or British?' Unless the expert user is one of those exceptional language learners who can sound as if they were raised in Buckinghamshire or Birmingham (Alabama), the authors always answer, 'Neither! You have a wonderful ___ accent', filling in the blank with the native language of the questioner. Although it is frequently assumed that many students would desire to reach native levels of pronunciation, Sung (2013) observed students in Hong Kong whose idealized models of English were often non-native speakers who had attained a high level of fluency. The students Sung spoke with did not always see NSs as reliable models of the English, both for reasons of comprehensibility and for identity reasons, i.e. not wanting to associate with present and past colonialism and imperialism (2013). In circumstances like this, it's obvious that students are already taking ownership of the language as they decide how they want to represent themselves in it.

Whether a more native-like accent will provide credibility to its speaker, or whether or not a native-like accent can truly

Activity 6.6

Is EFL/EIL having an effect on pronunciation teaching in your learning/teaching environment? If so, what effect is EFL/EIL having?

exist in a context that recognizes English as an International Language and the legitimacy of multiple Englishes, English teachers will have to decide what issues to focus most on with their students. Whether this will occur in an ESL, EFL, ELF, EIL or World Englishes context, the focus will be adopting a variety of English that most matches the direct needs of the students in their environment.

Suggested Readings

Graddol, D. (2006) English Next: Why Global English May Mean the End of "English as a Foreign Language"' (London: British Council).
http://englishagenda.britishcouncil.org/sites/ec/files/books-english-next.pdf
Although this free 132-page monograph is already ten years old, it is still the most important introduction to the still-changing role of the Englishes. Using excellent examples and data, Professor Graddol shows us how English has become the world's language. Written in an accessible style, this booklet should be read by anyone still not sure that English is the Lingua Franca of the modern world and also by those who need more evidence to convince others, such as curriculum developers and programme coordinators.

Jenkins, J. (2008) 'English as a Lingua Franca', PowerPoint presentation, JACET 47th Annual Convention, Shinjuku, Japan. http://www.jacet.org/2008convention/JACET2008_keynote_jenkins.pdf
This is the PowerPoint that Professor Jenkins, the leading researcher in the pronunciation of ELF, used for a plenary address in 2008. It can be used a quick review for what was discussed in this chapter. More importantly, it provides many examples of the influence and effects of EIL.

CHAPTER 7 # Technology and Pronunciation Teaching

This chapter first examines the history of the use and misuse of technology in teaching pronunciation and asks teachers to determine how they best think technology can be used to help students. Then, teachers are shown how new technologies can provide better understanding of how to teach pronunciation and how teachers themselves can become better researchers. Finally, the chapter asks teachers to reflect on how new technologies, including mobile technology, speech recognition software and phonetics/phonology websites can be used appropriately to help students both understand and produce language.

It always is difficult to write about developments in technology because the field is developing so rapidly that by the time a book comes to press, the innovations discussed are already passé; however, it is possible to consider a few essentials. From the previous chapters, it should be clear that for most of the PAYs we encounter, pronunciation instruction should focus on intelligibility rather than on any attempt to imitate the almost mythical native speaker accent.

The next question might be, 'Is technology enough of a solution for all of our pronunciation difficulties? Or is technology always going to be a "handmaiden" to human instruction?' For those who fear that the corporate education forces will try to replace all language teachers with auto tutors, computer programs or perhaps even neural implants in a few years, here is a story that should be calming.

Foreign language learning has always been something of an afterthought in American education. In Chapter 4, we read about the 1929 Coleman Report that said there was no real reason to teach spoken languages at that time. Today, we face a world in which (some variety of) English is everywhere. Even in Paris, once a stronghold of linguistic nationalism, the first author now has a hard time convincing younger people to speak in French once they find out he is American, even though his French is usually much better than their English. Such behaviour by the French would have been impossible when he first went to France in 1971. Now, however, there are indeed French teens who speak fluent English as a Lingua Franca so that they can communicate with their peers throughout the world. Yes, it seemed as though language learning in the United States was doomed to a tragic, slow, lingering death. But perhaps not.

In 1992, a small company released their product on CD-ROM under the name Rosetta Stone®. As their website explains, their core belief is that language learning should be natural and that interactive technology can provide the immersion needed (Official Rosetta Stone, 2016). Now worth almost US$300 million, Rosetta Stone is the clear commercial leader in CALL (computer-assisted language learning) in the United States. Despite its commercial success, something interesting happened to Rosetta Stone a few years ago that seems to indicate that CALL isn't quite all that is needed. Rosetta Stone began offering online tutoring sessions with live humans, called, appropriately, Live Tutoring, to make sure customers knew they were not just paying for more technology. Apparently, interactive technology alone isn't enough (Official Rosetta Stone, 2016).

Our jobs are safe. But our jobs will change in form for sure. People like people, even if they prefer to speak to them through a computer or a mobile device. In the end, we want to know there is a human out there. We have seen this also with responses to automated telephone menus for banking or plane reservations; we want to talk to a human.

It is also difficult to write about technology because that word is famously slippery. Are blackboard and chalk examples

Activity 7.1

1. Describe the typical level of access to technology in your learning/teaching context.
2. What technological tools have you used or been taught with?

of technology? In a lesser-developed country where basic schools are a luxury, the whiteboard would be a stunning technological advance, although the school might not have enough money to continue to buy whiteboard markers. Even in these 'impoverished' environments, we may be surprised at the 'modern' technological resources available to certain individuals or in certain areas in a country.

For example, the first author worked on a multi-year ESP project in Peru and Bolivia that was designed to help 'the poorest of the poor', such as street vendors. These street vendors were trying to sell their handiwork and crafts near tourist sites and major hotels. They needed to learn just enough English to be able to interact with the European, Japanese and American tourists. Intelligibility and comprehensibility were the major goals according to the needs analysis (Hall, Diaz, Alvarez and Arrol, 2013).

At first, the author was quite shocked when he realized that most of the street vendors, many of whom were functionally illiterate, had mobile phones that could be used as pedagogical devices. In fact, there is a 110 per cent 'penetration' of the mobile market in Peru as of 2016 (some people have multiple phones). That figure hides the fact that 20 per cent of the country's population has no access at all, while urban dwellers might have multiple phones (Budde, 2016). In this environment, it might make more sense to build apps rather than write books for most learners. Even the book is still a modern invention for some. Remember that the simple movable-type book was perhaps the most important technological advance in the history of humanity and was not 'invented' in Europe until around 1440 C.E.

Once again, we must stress that a proper needs analysis that shows us the correct PAY (purpose, audience and you – the teacher) is the crucial first step before any mention of technology. In other words, do not buy anything until you know what you need. We have seen too many beautiful language labs sitting in boxes in too many countries because there is no room for them; there is no faculty who knows how to use them; or there is no money for maintenance. All too often, language departments and teachers want to adopt technology that doesn't truly meet their needs. Sales reps are called sales reps, not advice reps, for very good reasons.

Regardless of the technology, tools serve the basic functions. Whether it's the audio-lingual lab of the 1960s and 1970s with tape recorders, or language-learning apps of today, the essentials are basically the same. The point is to draw the students' attention to aspects of speech production in an effort to help language students learn languages. Of course, just what learning a language means has changed from the 'near-native' goal of the ALM to the 'just good enough to be understood' of CLT.

In theory, teachers can focus attention on both students' receptive skills, such as being able to discriminate between phonemes that are new to them, as well as on productive skills, offering feedback on the individual production of utterances. Some major developments have also occurred in the role that technology can play in language instruction: the speech recognition and visualization of today offers much more in terms of individual feedback than the records and tapes of language labs in years past, in theory.

Activity 7.2

1. Describe how you have used technology to learn or teach a language.
2. What helped?
3. What hindered your progress?

Nonetheless, the authors wish to emphasize the past 50,000–100,000 years of language development have shown that no technology, not even a book, is necessary for successful pronunciation. Of course, correct and appropriate use of technology can be extremely useful, but never essential.

A Brief History of Technology in Pronunciation

The history of technology in pronunciation instruction, and in second language teaching for that matter, can be tied to both the development of technology and the development of language teaching methods. We can't be sure what first technologies were used to help teach or learn language, and specifically pronunciation. Perhaps they were clay tablets, wax tablets or symbols in the sand. Clearly, one of the first technologies was 'neuron based'; that isn't a real term but sounds very technological. Remember that some of the first language-learning texts that we still have were written (down) to help teach the correct pronunciation of Sanskrit for religious reasons, but before they were written down, they were memorized by using the same memory techniques (technology) that were used to memorize long epics, family lineages and laws in oral cultures. These astonishing memory 'tricks' were perhaps the first technology.

Likewise, we can be sure that there was intense language learning and teaching with emphasis on intelligibility as Buddhist monks from India were sent as far away as China by 250 B.C.E. to convert the Chinese. This was most likely the first intense wave of what would later be re-invented as the Communicative Approach.

What happened between then and when Comenius published modern language learning textbooks in the late 1600s, when most language learning was based on the Grammar-Translation that paid little attention to pronunciation? Sadly, Comenius' brilliant suggestions did not take hold, and education slipped back to memorizing forms and translating dead chunks of text.

Finally, with the advent of the Direct Method (see Chapter 4) at the end of the nineteenth century, pronunciation was again brought to the forefront of language teaching. Here technology consisted of many objects (realia) and an energetic teacher. Interestingly, another major technological advance, still used today in teaching pronunciation and listening, appeared concurrently: the phonograph in 1877. We don't actually use the phonograph anymore, but we do use its descendants. It appears that it was instantly used by some to teach language. The first line of a 1918 article reads, 'The use of the talking machine in teaching foreign languages is by no means new' (Clarke, 1918). Professor Clarke, then teaching French at Yale, notes that then most teachers thought it was simply too much bother to use the phonograph, but he feels that with proper preparation it can be very useful. Oddly, though, he ends with a statement on the use of this 'modern' technology that reflects an attitude still prevalent today: 'The writer ... does not introduce it ... in the earliest stages of instruction' (Clarke, 1918). Yes, even as early as 1918, it seemed that pronunciation training was not for the beginners. Of course, phonographs changed very quickly from the cylinders that Professor Clarke began to use as early as 1906, to records, cassette tapes, CDs and the digital audio files of today.

During the audio-lingual movement (WWII through the 1960s), a great deal of attention was paid to correct pronunciation. Most of this focus, however, was simply on the repetition of the teacher or audiotapes. The idea was that repetition would lead to familiarity, and learners could be trained to identify and distinguish between phonemes. It was also thought that in addition to focusing on individual sounds, these exercises could lead to more familiarity with connected speech. It was during this period that language labs became prominent, and students often spent time there 'discriminating between members of minimal pairs' (Larsen-Freeman and Anderson, 2013, p. 46). Indeed, the first author remembers spending hours in the language labs practising the four nasal vowels of French ('un bon vin blanc'), which he still uses even though most speakers of French now only use three. 'I worked hard to get those four sounds; I'm not giving them up!' is what he says when confronted by speakers of Modern French about his dated pronunciation.

After the Chomsky revolution and the downfall of the Behaviourists with their parroting, the so-called designer methods (Cognitive Code Learning, Community Language Learning, Suggestopedia, Silent Way, etc.) took a different approach to language teaching and pronunciation instruction. The Silent Way used charts to introduce model pronunciation and allowed students to recognize target pronunciation before ever having to produce sounds for themselves. Likewise, **Total Physical Response** (TPR) does not require pronunciation practice as it is learned receptively; students are not expected to speak in the beginning, and thereby the method honours the 'Silent Period' of language acquisition.

Unlike the Audio-lingual Method, the Communicative Approach placed less focus on accuracy than it did on intelligibility and what was perhaps misleadingly called fluency. Even though student textbooks increasingly came with companion CDs or even websites, the teaching of pronunciation since the start of the Communicative Approach has often been overlooked. There are numerous causes for this, primarily with regard to a lack of training, experience and confidence on the part of teachers. Another reason for this is a perceived lack of time to focus on pronunciation instruction in the language classroom. Regardless, pronunciation plays a central role in a speaker's intelligibility and a listener's comprehension, so it is not something that can be disregarded. Much of teachers' tendency to gloss over pronunciation instruction can also be seen as a rejection of the endless drilling that came with the Audio-lingual Method and language labs. When focusing on pronunciation, teachers using the Communicative Approach have tended to focus more on prosody and suprasegmentals than individual sound or segmental features.

Post-methods approaches, such as Content-Based Instruction (CBI) and Task-Based Language Teaching (TBLT) as well as ESP courses, may not explicitly focus on pronunciation instruction as 'teachers must balance the needs of their students within a somewhat fixed curriculum. If this is the case, pronunciation is not always explicitly included even in a speaking course, and teachers need to find ways to integrate pronunciation into existing curriculum and textbook materials' (Celce-Murcia et al., 2010, p. 381). This is not to say that there is not room for explicit pronunciation instruction in the classroom; in fact, 'it is often covered in class slots divorced from the rest of the syllabus' (Brown, 2008, p. 203) instead of being incorporated into other aspects of the class. It is this much-needed inclusion of pronunciation instruction and feedback with which technology can help, especially in terms of offering students individual instruction and feedback.

In the past twenty years, as computers, tablets and mobile devices have become increasingly affordable and available, and access to the Internet has become almost ubiquitous, Computer-Assisted Language Learning (CALL) has grown to include mobile-assisted language learning. CALL is of interest to language teachers and learners because it can provide individualized instruction and immediate feedback on the correctness of a learner's response to computerized tasks (Nagata, 1993). As CALL is adapted for use in pronunciation teaching, it is most commonly referred to as computer-aided pronunciation instruction (CAP) or computer-assisted pronunciation teaching (CAPT) although these terms are not yet well known. Rogerson-Revell (2011, p. 259) points out that although technology is

Activity 7.3

Have you tried using a language learning app? Explain how it worked. Was it effective? Why or why not? If you haven't tried such an app, find a review of an app online, and summarize the review for your classmates either orally or in writing, as directed by your instructor.

increasingly being used in language and pronunciation teaching, researchers like Levis (2006) still find that it has not reached its full potential.

New Developments in Technology and Pronunciation Teaching

Technology can be utilized in various aspects of teaching pronunciation, such as drawing students' attention to segmental errors as well as prosody issues (intonation, stress, etc.). In addition to helping students recognize and identify sounds in the target language, technology can help with students' language production. Since audio and video recording devices on cell phones, computers, and so on, are now ubiquitous and within reach of most students, it makes sense for teachers to incorporate them into pronunciation instruction. Even the act of recording and listening to short bursts of one's own speech is enough to draw attention to the difference between perceived and actual sounds. In ESL environments, the same technology can be used to record differences in the accents of native speakers to help destroy the myth of monolithic English.

Models of Pronunciation

Technology can be employed at the most basic level of pronunciation instruction by demonstrating target sounds as well as the place and manner of pronunciation. As we have already mentioned, this is by no means a new invention. Language labs and even the simple phonograph provided something very similar. However, there have been many improvements with the Internet and mobile applications. Before we share any resources, we'd like to note that we are purposefully leaving out any resources that must be paid for. Many publishers provide excellent resources to accompany their textbooks, and there are a number of useful websites and programs that can be purchased, but our experience has shown us that when there is a lack of institutional funding, these resources are out of reach for teachers who cannot afford to spend their own money. For that reason, we've only chosen to feature free resources, and we are extremely grateful for the people who are generous to share their work with the world.

First of all, we can take something such as Merriam-Webster's Learners Dictionary (http://www.learnersdictionary.com) and the Howjsay (http://howjsay.com) free online Talking Dictionary of English Pronunciation to give learners a reliable model for isolated words on their vocabulary lists. If we are working at the level of isolated phonemes, the website of the International Phonetic Association has resources available for learning the sounds of the IPA chart (http://www.internationalphoneticassociation.org/), as does the British Council, which has an interactive online version and a free downloadable version of the phonemic chart for the sounds of English (http://www.teachingenglish.org.uk/article/phonemic-chart). A very useful tool for teachers and students is the University of Iowa's Sounds of American English website and companion mobile app (http://soundsofspeech.uiowa.edu/). Not only do the website and app give model phonemes, they also give a video and a detailed diagram to demonstrate how to make the sound. One website which is the companion website for a commercial textbook is Ship or Sheep (http://www.shiporsheep.com), which provides online practice with minimal pairs. Offering the best of both of these worlds is Sharon Widmayer and Holly Gray's Sounds of English Website (http://www.soundsofenglish.org), which offers demonstrations of sounds, diagrams of their articulation, minimal pairs and activities for students and teachers alike. English Corner's Pronunciation page (http://www.englishcorner.vacau.com/pronunciation/pronunciation.html) offers packages of sounds and activities that can be downloaded and used offline by both teachers and students.

The websites mentioned above primarily deal with individual sounds and words in isolation, which is fine for lower level students, but these also lack context and the flow of connected speech. Two interesting websites that offer speech in context are Voice of America's Learning English website, which offers news articles that are written at a lower level than most news reports, making them accessible to learners. The articles are accompanied by an audio track, so learners can listen and read at the same time. It should be mentioned that the tracks play at a slower level than most unscripted speech. Once learners are ready to hear more speech in context, we would advise moving to more authentic sources like the BBC, NPR, CNN, and so on.

For students and teachers interested in different English accents, George Mason University has compiled The Speech Accent Archive, which has audio samples of sentences in English being spoken by speakers from around the world. It is an interesting resource for both teachers and students because it is a collection of native and non-native speakers. For teachers in training or teachers preparing to work with a new demographic of English language students, it offers generalizations of different regions' speech patterns.

Analysing Students' Pronunciation

Of course, students will want more than just model forms of pronunciation. They will need and want feedback on their individual performance, which can be time consuming for teachers. For years, many language programs like Rosetta Stone have provided their customers with the ability to record and visualize their speech in waves or pitch contours so that they can compare their speech to a target model. Rosetta Stone is a bit expensive, and waveform analysis has some limitations in that it's not always possible for learners to know exactly where their speech differs from the target model. There are free programs that visualize learners' speech, such as the SIL (Summer Institute of Linguistics) International's suite of Speech Tools, including the Speech Analyzer (http://www-01.sil.org/computing/sa/index.htm), which gives acoustic analysis of speech sounds; the Phonology Assistant (http://phonologyassistant.sil.org/download/), which helps chart and manage sounds recorded with the Speech Analyzer; and, appropriately named, IPA Help (http://www-01.sil.org/computing/ipahelp/index.htm), which helps students hear and transcribe the different sounds of the IPA chart. The KTH Royal Institute of Technology's School of Computer Science and Communication offers a similar program to the Speech Analyzer, called Wavesurfer (https://sourceforge.net/projects/wavesurfer/), a useful tool for sound visualization. The University College of London's Faculty of Brain Sciences offers a similar collection of applications and online resources (http://www.phon.ucl.ac.uk/resource/software.php) for teaching pronunciation and for phonetics research.

With so many students in all parts of the world carrying around mobile devices, it only makes sense that these should be employed in the classroom. For those with smartphones, there are many speech-to-text programs that come with no extra charge. Both Microsoft and Apple offer speech recognition software, which can be particularly useful when students are working on vocabulary lists. The benefit of these programs is that students have unlimited chances to get instantaneous feedback on their speech. There is a limitation with this, however, in that it doesn't necessarily explain students' errors.

More useful than the text-to-speech capabilities of smartphones are their ability to record and store audio. Students can record their own personal speaking journals to share with their teacher or can offer responses to class questions, introduce themselves or even record speeches to keep a record of their progress or to share with other students. Through a class website or podcast, or by simply e-mailing audio files to teachers, teachers can give feedback on their progress. This, however, does take some time and effort on the teacher's part, but it is convenient.

Activity 7.4

A Parting Question
As we move into the final chapter, we'd like to ask you to consider what role technology can play in pronunciation instruction in your context. Does it PAY?

Suggested Readings

As we mentioned in the chapter, it is dangerous to recommend sites or articles about technology, since, almost by definition, technology changes so quickly.

Levis, J. (2007) Computer Technology in Teaching and Researching Pronunciation, *Annual Review of Applied Linguistics*, 27, 184–202. http://www.u.arizona.edu/~piskula/TeachingPronWithTech.pdf
As an overview article about how pronunciation can be assisted by computer technology, this article can serve as a blueprint for looking at continuing developments. Rather than slavishly following the specific programs or apps in this article, you should look at how they are analysed, and use that as a model for your own analysis of how computers, smartphones and that as yet un-invented device can help you and your students.

CHAPTER 8 **Conclusion**

Just the Facts

In this text, you've learned about the basic building blocks of spoken language, the sounds; that was phonetics. From there we saw how sounds can and can't be combined, depending on the language; we call that phonotactics. Then we introduced the idea of the mental representation of significant sounds in a specific language; we discovered phonemes. We looked at how the sounds interact as a system: phonology brought the parts all together.

Using what we had learned about the segmentals, we put them together and watched what happened; you actually heard the allophones of English most likely for the first time. And finally, we looked at how elements larger than individual sounds work together to form prosody and create a type of personality for each language. In total, you learned a great deal about how pronunciation works.

And Now the Complications

Even though we have a good grasp of the sound system and the production of sounds, syllables and sentences, we still have no simple answer to what, when and how we should teach pronunciation. In fact, sometimes we're not even sure whom we should teach.

In Chapter 4, we examined how the traditional trove of quantitative research available for many aspects of language learning was never developed for pronunciation studies.

Instead, most work was based on anecdotal reports from a few gifted teachers who had good ideas that worked for many people. However, we kept returning to the necessity of the needs analysis for pronunciation instruction. We introduced the idea of PAY as shorthand for the results of a needs analysis. Understand, and then plan. We must discover the purpose that our particular audience needs and then temper our methods with the reality of what we as instructors can do. What works for you may not work for me, and certainly vice versa.

Our mild dismay at the paucity of hard research that we learned about in Chapter 4 became even more important as we examined the changing role of English globally in Chapter 6. It became clear that English no longer belongs to any particular group. As a result, it's hard for us to maintain that a particular variety of English pronunciation should be pushed as *the* standard. Rather, there are many standards depending on the PAY.

In Chapter 7, we looked briefly at the myth of the robo-teacher that is going to replace all of us any day now with the absolute patience of the electronic brain and with no wild demands for minimum wage. Instead it turns out that the best available technology still works better when coupled with human interaction. Human interaction is still the best, the same as when humans first began teaching each other languages long before history began.

Activity 8.1

The information we presented is essential and helpful, but now we turn the discussion over to you and ask you what you will do to incorporate more pronunciation into your own language teaching. Ah, you're right; our first question should be: do I need to even bother with pronunciation instruction, or is it a waste of time?

Activity 8.2

Let's go through our ten 'rules' and see how you will use that information to continue to learn and grow. These little vignettes and questions should make you uncomfortable at first but in the end will give you the sense of freedom that a teacher should have. We hope you are able to discuss these in class and have some very lively discussions.

Ten Rules to Guide the Way

In the Western tradition, we always have ten answers or five answers. We're told it's because we have five fingers on each hand. And it most likely is. Likewise, our ability to speak is based on very physical traits that delimit what is humanly possible. It would be useless to have ultrasonic sounds as part of a human language since our human ears can't interpret them. There are hard facts: we can't (normally) produce labio-dental stops. There are also universal trends: when segments interact, there is often assimilation. The rest is all open to interpretation and variation.

1. **Some features of an L2 accent have no effect on intelligibility.**
   (a) How will you determine what features do have an effect on intelligibility? Are you the type who is organized enough to keep a database or journal of the mistakes or errors that you hear or even produce? One of the authors is; the other author knows that is not in his future.
   (b) Can you research the possible problems that your students might have? Well, that is easy if you have a homogeneous group. It wouldn't take that much effort to find out which segments or combinations might be difficult for most Arabic speakers. Well, that is true until you learn that Egyptian Arabic speakers have slightly different issues than Saudi speakers do.

(c) And what do you do if you are teaching German as a Second Language to immigrants from twelve different countries and five different language families?
(d) Do you have to wait until your students make the proverbial mistakes, or can you pre-empt them and teach something they might not need? How can you plan a syllabus around what might happen?

2. **Not everything we notice needs to be fixed.**
   (a) Are you able to just let a mistake slide if it doesn't affect intelligibility? Franz says, 'I left it on the bet.' Can you keep yourself from immediately correcting him with 'Bed – you mean bed'?
   (b) And can you determine what does need to be fixed? Is intelligibility the only criterion that is important in your PAY?

3. **Research can help us determine which features influence intelligibility the most.**
   Do you really believe that? How will you access research? And then how will you evaluate research? Will you be able to determine if the research conclusions match your PAY? Which types of research do you trust? Which researchers?

4. **Most adults will not learn to speak a new language without a 'foreign' accent.**
   (a) Now this is an easy one, usually. What do you do, however, when an insistent student wants to speak just like a native? What do you tell him or her? What advice can you give this person?
   (b) A student asks you about a company that guarantees to 'reduce' her or his accent for only a few thousand dollars. Your response? Or do you open up your own accent reduction service?
   (c) Your school principal asks you about hiring a non-native English teacher. The principal is worried because the new teacher has an 'accent'. And?

5. **Learning to speak (i.e. literally pronounce) an L2 takes more than just cognitive ability and is therefore very different**

from learning reading, grammar, vocabulary or even listening. It's physical in addition to cognitive.
   (a) What techniques can you use, develop or modify that help your students with the physical aspects of pronunciation?
   (b) What social restrictions might be involved? How would you teach pronunciation to, for example, a group of Islamic women who are completely veiled, if you are a man or the class is mixed?
   (c) Which groups are more likely to enjoy 'silly' pronunciation games? Would any of your students be embarrassed by making mistakes in class? Are you comfortable playing silly games to emphasize the physical nature of pronunciation?

6. **(Brief) targeted feedback ('correction') is what works best.**
   (a) What does brief mean to you? To your students? How many different feedback techniques do you know, and which ones can you use with which students? Which ones can't you use?
   (b) How many brief feedback moments are too many for a class? For a student? What if one of your students really has severe intelligibility problems, but the others are fine?

7. **Learners need to hear authentic language too.**
   (a) If you are a native speaker, are you comfortable giving up control of the class? Why should you play tapes, watch videos or listen to songs when students have you as their model?
   (b) If you are a non-native speaker, are you good enough to be considered 'authentic'? Does it matter? What do you do about your own 'pronunciation shortcomings'?

8. **The L1 of a speaker has major influences on success in pronouncing an L2.**
   (a) As a teacher, how do you deal with the fact that stereotypically some L1 speakers will just naturally be 'better' than other L1 speakers? How do you evaluate the different groups knowing the basic unfairness of the process?
   (b) As a language learner, how do you deal with the fact that you most likely will never be 'a native speaker' simply because of your L1?

9. **Many of the most important factors that influence success are outside the control of the teacher and the learner.**
   Can you accept failure? What does failure mean to you? Can you claim success? What is success for you? What can you do about the factors outside your control?

10. **It all depends on the PAY.**
    Well, sure it depends on the PAY, but let's say again that the *Y* in PAY is really what matters. And how will you continue to learn so that pronunciation has an appropriate place in modern language teaching?

    What have we forgotten? What have you learned or want to learn that we didn't mention? You know this is just the start of what you will learn about teaching and not teaching pronunciation. Will you share that with others in papers, workshops, conferences or even just peer-to-peer conversations? It's time for the student to become the teacher. Thank you and we look forward to learning from you.

Suggested Readings

We are not going to recommend any readings since what comes next has not yet been written. Rather, we suggest (almost insist) that you become part of the conversation by attending workshops, videoconferences or even by arranging your own local meetings.

To help, you should think about joining one of the two major international organizations or their local affiliates. More importantly, you should think about contributing your own ideas, techniques and questions. Each of you has something important to say.

- TESOL International: http://www.tesol.org/connect
- International Association of Teachers of English as a Foreign Language (IATEFL): http://www.iatefl.org/

Glossary

accent A distinguishing manner of speech based primarily on pronunciation, particularly one connected to a location, ethnicity or social class (does not refer to grammar or vocabulary).

accent modification The preferred term for the process of altering one's pronunciation to more closely match that of a new language or dialect. Although the term is often used interchangeably with **accent reduction**, it is a preferable term because *accent reduction* places a value judgement on accents that deviate from an imagined standard.

accent reduction See **accent modification**.

acquisition versus **learning** The distinction between the development and internalization of language (acquisition), usually by infants and small children, versus the conscious study of the forms of language (learning) undertaken by children and adults.

affricate A phoneme that merges a stop with fricative. Whether it is perceived as two sounds or one depends on the specific language. The [č] in *church* in English is one sound for native speakers of English while the same sound (but transcribed as [tʃ]) in German or French is heard as two sounds by those speakers. Compare that with [ts], which is one sound in German as in *zehn* ('ten') but two in English as in *cats*.

allophone Any of the sounds that are realized from a single phoneme; allophones are predictable based on context. For example, in most American accents, the intervocalic /t/ becomes the flap [D] before an unstressed syllable; contrast *retain* and *butter*.

alveolar ridge The gum ridge behind and above the upper teeth.

alveopalatal Consonants articulated with the tongue behind the alveolar ridge and raised towards the palate.

approximant A consonant produced with one articulator close to another without touching it. It includes the semivowels and the liquids.

articulatory phonetics The subfield of phonetics that describes how sounds are produced. Compare with *acoustic phonetics*, the physical characteristics of sounds, such as frequencies, and *auditory phonetics*, the study of the perception of speech sounds.

articulatory setting The default position of the mouth when a sound is produced; specific to each language/dialect/accent.

aspiration A puff of air following a sound. In English, [p, t, k], the voiceless stops, are aspirated in initial position. Represented by an apostrophe for mild aspiration and by a raised *h* for stronger aspiration: [p'] and [pʰ].

assimilation Adapting a phoneme to make it similar to a sound before or after it.

Audio-lingual Method A teaching method based on behaviourism that focuses on listening, drilling and repetition of target speech patterns. Great emphasis was placed on 'native-like' pronunciation.

broad transcription Transcription that focuses on the most immediately noticeable features of an utterance. Contrasted with **narrow transcription**.

Comenius, John Amos A seventeenth-century Czech philosopher and teacher who was an early innovator in language education.

complementary distribution The occurrence of speech sounds in mutually exclusive contexts.

comprehensible input (CI) part of the **Input Hypothesis** put forward by Stephen Krashen, CI is input that is just beyond a learner's level of competence, but not beyond his or her level of understanding. Krashen hypothesizes that CI is essential for language acquisition.

comprehensibility How much work the *listener* must do to understand the speaker. Contrast with **intelligibility**, how much the *listener* understands.

consonant Basic class of sounds made by obstructing the airflow through the vocal tract. Contrast with **vowel** and **approximant**.

consonant cluster Two or more consonants occurring within a single syllable that are not separated by a vowel.

Critical Age Hypothesis Also referred to as the *Critical Period Hypothesis*, the hypothesis that if one does not acquire a language before/around puberty, she or he will face more difficulty in learning the language natively after the age has been reached. Also assumed that native-like pronunciation is almost impossible for anyone learning a language after the critical age.

Czech language A Slavic language spoken in the Czech Republic closely related to Slovak and other Slavic languages such as Russian or Polish. Word-intial stress is predictable in Czech, and it also has phonemic vowel length in contrast to English.

deep structure In transformational grammar, the underlying structure or representation of the meaning of an utterance. Contrasted to **surface structure**, which is what is written/spoken.

descriptive linguistics An approach to linguistics concerned with language as it is used without judgement, in contrast to **prescriptive linguistics**, which seeks to set standards for appropriate and proper language.

devoicing To pronounce a voiced consonant without vibrating the vocal cords. Final devoicing occurs in many languages; [b, v, d, g, z] become [p, f, t, k, s], for example.

diaeresis A sign used to show the separation of adjoining vowels into separate syllables. Compare *Aïda*, which has three syllables. Still used by the famous publication *The New Yorker* in place of the hyphen for the same purpose, for example *coöperate*.

digraph A combination of two letters that represents a single sound, such as *th*, *ph*, *ch* and *sh* in English.

diphthong Two vowel sounds articulated in combination and perceived as one vowel sound. *Boy*, *about* and *house* demonstrate the three non-predictable (i.e. phonemic) diphthongs in English. Other non-predictable diphthongs exist in other languages.

emic Different and significant. Contrast with *etic*, different but not necessarily significant.

English as a Lingua Franca (ELF) The use of English as a common language between speakers of different languages. No reference to 'native speakers'; said to now be the most common form of English used today.

English as an International Language (EIL) The use of English as a common language between speakers of different languages, including native speakers of English, similar to **English as a Lingua Franca**.

etic Observably different, but not necessarily significant. Contrast with *emic*.

flap A consonant produced when the tongue quickly strikes the alveolar ridge in English, although other types of flaps are possible in other languages; compare with *trill* which is a vibration of the tongue (or other part of the mouth) by the airstream as in the Spanish trill written as the double *rr* in *perro* ('dog') that contrasts with the flap written as a single *r* in *pero* ('but').

fossilized Used to describe a language learner who has stopped learning. The learner usually has reached a level of proficiency sufficient to meet the learner's needs and wants. Any attempt at additional improvement seems to trigger the law of diminishing returns.

free variation When two sounds can be substituted for each other without any change in meaning. Compare the two pronunciations of *often* with and without the /t/.

fricative A consonant made by obstructing the flow of air in the mouth and producing considerable, audible friction, such as [f, v, s, z, š, ž] in English.

functional load The relative importance of phonemes to communicate meaning in utterances. The load is not only based on phonemes but also on position. Thus phoneme X might be unimportant finally but very important initially, such as is the case for b/p.

glide Also called a **semivowel**, a sound produced similar to a vowel that occurs at the onset or final of a syllable but that is perceived by native speakers as a consonant.

glottal A voiced or voiceless sound produced in opening of the vocal cords in the larynx.

grammar translation An approach to teaching language that involves students learning grammatical rules and using them to translate sentences between their L1 and L2. Pronunciation is often neglected.

hypercorrection Over-applying a rule by children or adults, for example the child's 'goed' based on the rule 'Add –*ed* to the infinitive to form the past tense.' The child has never heard this form (we hope) but creates it once he or she has 'discovered' the past tense rule. Usually the child returns to the correct form; that is not the case all the time for adult learners or even native speakers, who many continue to use hypercorrect forms for perceived status reasons, such as 'She gave the book to Cinderella and I [*sic*] for our anniversary.' Hypercorrection is also indicative that a language change may be underway.

hyperliteracy A neologism by the authors referring to the perception by educated speakers that the written form is the norm-giving rather than the original spoken form. Leads to spelling pronunciations and sometimes hypercorrections.
initial At the beginning of a syllable.
Input Hypothesis Stephen Krashen's hypothesis that in order for acquisition to take place, a language learner must receive comprehensible input (CI) based on contextual cues or schemata that trigger a connection for the learner.
intelligibility How much the *listener* understands. Contrast with **comprehensibility**, how much work the *listener* must do to understand the speaker.
interdental A consonant produced by placing the tongue between the teeth [ð, θ].
International Phonetic Alphabet (IPA) A system of transcribing sounds of languages where each sound is represented by one symbol and each symbol represents one sound. Unfortunately, there are many variants in use for historical reasons.
intonation The rise and fall of connected speech.
IPA See **International Phonetic Alphabet**.
labial A sound produced at the lips.
labiodental A sound produced with the lower lip in contact with the upper teeth.
labiovelar A sound produced by simultaneous rounding the lips and tightening the velum.
lateral Usually a liquid /l/ articulated with air flowing over one or both sides of the tongue.
lax Sounds pronounced with relaxed vocal muscles. Contrast to *tense*.
learning versus **acquisition** The conscious study of the forms of language (learning) versus the automatic, innate ability of the typical child to 'pick up' any language for which he or she received sufficient input.
lexical stress The emphasis given to a particular syllable or syllables within a word.
lightning drill A teachable-moment, very short drill that is used only when needed.
Lingua Franca Core (LFC) Proposed by Jennifer Jenkins, pronunciation features that seem to be singificaant in effective and efficient communication in an ELF environment.

linguistic exogamy Marriage practice that requires that spouses come from different language communities.
liquid Usually a subset of approximants. In English the lateral /l/ and rhotic /r/ that behave in similar ways.
medial A sound occurring in the middle of a word. Contrast with *initial* and *final*.
minimal pair Two words distinguished by one different phoneme, for example *bat* versus *pat*. The gold standard for determining the phonemic status of any given sound contrast.
narrow transcription Transcription that focuses all of the acoustic features of an utterance. Contrast with **broad transcription.**
nasal A sound produced by opening the nasal cavity and stopping the airflow through the oral cavity.
natural classes Groups of sounds that behave similarly, for example the liquids or the voiceless stops.
off-glide A glide produced after the articulation of another sound, used to describe the second vowel in a diphthong. Can be represented in many ways, for example [aʊ] or /aw/.
palate The hard roof of the mouth.
parole Actual linguistic behaviour in practice, in contrast to the established linguistic system.
PAY A mnemonic for a quick needs analysis of any class: purpose, audience and you, the teacher.
phone Base meaning sound as in telephone, phonograph, phonemic, phonetic.
phoneme The smallest unpredictable, significant unit of language sound.
phonemic awareness The ability to hear and identify different phonemes.
phonemic inventory All of the phonemes of an individual language. Each accent/dialect/language can have its own specific phonemic inventory.
phonemic transcription Recording in writing the significant sounds in speech.
phonetics The study of human speech sounds.
phonology The study of the systematic organization of speech sounds.
phonotactics The study of possible phoneme combinations.
prescriptive linguistics An approach to linguistics which seeks to set standards for appropriate and proper language, in contrast to

descriptive linguistics, which is concerned with language as it is used.
pronunciation The articulation of sounds.
prosody The suprasegmental properties of language.
prosthesis The addition of sound at the beginning of a word, such as [ɛspænɪš] for [spænɪš] by many Spanish learners of English.
Rassias Method A method of language teaching that places the learners at the centre of attention and encourages the use of theatrical devices to act out real-life situations.
Received Pronunciation (RP) The relatively modern 'British English' educated, non-regional accent. It was not 'universal' among the educated until the twentieth century and is in flux and losing ground to more class and regionally based forms. For most Americans, this is the form associated with British movies, the Royal Family and British series on PBS.
retroflex Sounds pronounced with the tongue curled towards the palate.
rhotic Accent/dialect where *r* is pronounced before consonants and at the ends of words. RP is non-rhotic while some British accents/dialects are rhotic. On the other hand, Standard American is rhotic while some accents/dialects ('Boston' and some Southern forms) are non-rhotic.
RP See **Received Pronunciation**.
rounding The rounding of the lips during the production of a vowel.
segmental The individual elements of speech.
semivowel A vowel that is used as a consonant. In English /y/ and /w/ in *yes* and *want*.
shibboleth A form or custom that serves as a marker of inclusion or exclusion. In linguistics, usually a pronunciation, a spelling or a lexical item. For example, the lack (or presence) of a period after the abbreviation of *mister* can be a shibboleth for distinguishing between British and American English: Mr versus Mr.
stop A sound produced by completely blocking the airflow in the vocal tract for a short period.
stress Emphasis placed on individual syllables in a word.
stress-timed language A language, such as English, German or Russian, in which syllables may be pronounced with different lengths of time according to whether they are stressed or not.

Contrast with **syllable-timed language**, such as French, where syllables are pronounced with a relatively equal amount of time regardless of their stress. This distinction is not accepted by all but is useful as a heuristic.

suprasegmental Features of language above the individual sounds, such as rhythm, and intonation. Contrast with **segmental**.

surface structure In transformational grammar, it is the individual words used to express an utterance's meaning. Contrast with **deep structure**, the underlying structure or representation of the meaning of an utterance.

syllable-timed language A language, such as French, where syllables are pronounced with a relatively equal amount of time regardless of their stress. Contrast with **stress-timed language**, such as English, in which syllables may be pronounced with different lengths of time depending on whether they are stressed or not. This distinction is not accepted by all but is useful as a heuristic.

tense A sound produced with tightened vocal muscles. Contrast with **lax**.

tone Intonation in an utterance.

TPR (Total Physical Response) Language teaching technique that focuses on coordinating physical movement and language acquisition by giving students ample opportunity to engage with a second language without the pressure of producing language at early stages of teaching.

trill A rapid vibration of the tongue (or other part of the mouth) by the airstream as in the Spanish trill written with double *rr* in the word *perro* ('dog') in contrast to the Spanish flap written with single *r* in the word *pero* ('but'); compare with flap which is a single striking of the tongue against another part of the mouth as in American [D] in *butter*.

umlaut A symbol that often marks the rounding of a front vowel (ü or ö) or simply the fronting of a vowel (ä); used in many European languages as part of their standard orthography. Contrast with the same symbol used as the diaeresis that signals two adjacent vowels that should be pronounced separately, as in *coöperate*, the form still used by the famous publication *The New Yorker*.

velar Sounds that are articulated at the back of the tongue raised towards the soft palate; also called velum.

voiced A sound produced with vibration in the vocal cords, such as all English vowels and [z] or [b]. Contrast with **voiceless**.

voiceless A sound produced without vibration in the vocal cords such as [s] or [p]. Contrast with **voiced**.

vowel A class of sounds made without an obstruction of the airflow in the vocal tract. Contrast with **consonant**.

vowel purity Vowels with no off-glides. Contrast Spanish [e:] with American [e^I]. So-called long vowels in English are actually diphthongs, but since the off-glide is predictable, the topic is not essential in discussions with native speakers. Because our so-called long vowels are actually diphthongs, vowel purity is a stumbling block for (most) English speakers learning another language if they are attempting to be 'native-like'. Of course, by the time you reach this definition in this book, you should know that goal is not usually attainable and the effort to achieve it is most likely a waste of time.

References

Acton, W. (1984) 'Changing Fossilized Pronunciation', *TESOL Quarterly*, 18(1), 71–85.
American Speech-Language-Hearing Association (n.d.) 'Accent Modification' (accessed 7 March 2016 from http://www.asha.org/public/speech/development/accent-modification/).
Avery, P. and E. Schmidt (1987) *The Teaching of Pronunciation: An Introduction for Teachers of English as a Second Language*, TESL Talk, Citizenship Development Branch, Ministry of Citizenship and Culture.
Bauer, L. (2015) 'Australian and New Zealand English', in M. Reed and J. Levis (eds) *The Handbook of English Pronunciation* (Kindle Edition) (New York: Wiley-Blackwell).
Brown, A. (2008) 'Pronunciation and Good Language Learners', in C. Griffiths (ed.) *Lessons from Good Language Learners* (Cambridge: Cambridge University Press), pp. 197–207.
Brutt-Griffler, J. (2006) 'Languages of Wider Communication', in K. Brown (ed.), *Encyclopedia of Language & Linguistics* (Amsterdam: Elsevier), pp. 690–97.
Budde, P. (2016) 'Peru – Mobile Infrastructure, Broadband, Operators – Statistics and Analyses', Budde Comm (accessed 8 March 2016 from http://www.budde.com.au/Research/Peru-Mobile-Infrastructure-Broadband-Operators-Statistics-and-Analyses.html).
Celce-Murcia, M., D. M. Brinton and J. M. Goodwin (1996) *Teaching Pronunciation: A Reference for Teachers of English to Speakers of Other Languages* (Cambridge: Cambridge University Press).
Celce-Murcia, M., D. M. Brinton and J. M. Goodwin (2010) *Teaching Pronunciation: A Reference for Teachers of English to Speakers of Other Languages* (Cambridge: Cambridge University Press).
Clarke, C. C. (1918) 'The Phonograph in Modern Language Teaching', *The Modern Language Journal*, 3(3), 116–22.
Coleman, A. (1929) *The Teaching of Modern Foreign Languages in the United States* (New York: MacMillan).

Crystal, D. (2003) *English as a Global Language* (New York: Cambridge University Press) (accessed August 20, 2016 from http://public.eblib.com/choice/publicfullrecord.aspx?p=221205).

Dalton-Puffer, C. and B. Seidlhofer (1994) *Pronunciation* (Oxford: Oxford University Press).

Darcy, I. (2015) *Powerful and Effective Pronunciation Instruction: How Can We Achieve It?* (accessed August 20, 2016 from http://www.upf.edu/masterlinguistica/_pdf/Pronunciation_Instruction_Darcy_June_2015_UPF.pdf).

Darcy, I., D. Ewert and R. Lidster (2012) 'Bringing Pronunciation Instruction Back into the Classroom: An ESL Teachers' Pronunciation "toolbox"', in J. Levis and K. LeVelle (eds) *Social Factors in Pronunciation Acquisition*, Proceedings of the 3rd Annual Pronunciation in Second Language Learning and Teaching Conference, Iowa State University, 16–17 September, pp. 93–108 (accessed August 20, 2016 from http://jlevis.public.iastate.edu/Proceedingsfrom3rdPSLLT.pdf).

Derwing, T. M. and M. J. Munro (2015) *Pronunciation Fundamentals: Evidence-based Perspectives for L2 Teaching and Research* (Amsterdam: John Benjamins Publishing).

Dochtery, G. and P. Foulkes (1999) 'Derby and Newcastle: Instrumental Phonetics and Variationist Studies', in P. Foulkes and G. Dochtery (eds) *Urban Voices* (New York: Routledge), pp. 47–71.

Doughty, C. J. and M. H. Long (2003) *The Handbook of Second Language Acquisition* (Malden, MA: Wiley-Blackwell).

Firth, J. R. (1956) 'Descriptive Linguistics and the Study of English', in F. R. Palmer (ed.) *Selected Papers of J. R. Firth 1952–1959* (Bloomington, IN: Indiana University Press).

Foote, J. A., A. K. Holtby and T. M. Derwing (2011) 'Survey of the Teaching of Pronunciation in Adult ESL Programs in Canada, 2010', *TESL Canada Journal*, 29(1), 1–22.

Friginal, E. (2009) *The Language of Outsourced Call Centers: A Corpus-based Study of Cross-cultural Interaction* (Amsterdam: John Benjamins Publishing).

Gilbert, J. B. (1984) *Clear Speech: Pronunciation and Listening Comprehension in North American English* (New York: Cambridge University Press).

Gilbert, J. B. (2008) *Teaching Pronunciation: Using the Prosody Pyramid* (New York: Cambridge University Press).

Gilbert, J. B. (2012) *Clear Speech: Pronunciation and Listening Comprehension in North American English* (New York: Cambridge University Press).

Graddol, D. (2003) 'The Decline of the Native Speaker' in G. Anderman and .M. Rogers (eds) *Translation Today: Trends and Perspectives* (Clevedon: Multilingual Matters), pp. 152–67.

Graddol, D. (2007) *English Next: Why Global English May Mean the End of English as a Foreign Language* (British Council (Plymouth: Latimer Trend & Co.).

Grant, L. J. and D. Brinton (2014) *Pronunciation Myths: Applying Second Language Research to Classroom Teaching* (Ann Arbor: University of Michigan Press).

Hall, C., A. Diaz, J. C. Alvarez and D. Arrol (2013) 'Helping the Poorest of the Poor in the Tourist Industry', TESOL 2013 International Convention & English Language Expo, 23 March, Dallas Texas.

Huttner-Koros, A. (2015) 'The Hidden Bias of Science's Universal Language', *The Atlantic*, 21 August (accessed August 20, 2016 from http://www.theatlantic.com/science/archive/2015/08/english-universal-language-science-research/400919/).

Jackson, J. E. (1983) *The Fish People: Linguistic Exogamy and Tukanoan Identity in Northwest Amazonia* (New York: Cambridge University Press).

Jackson, D. and J. Jacobs (2016) 'Trump Attacks Fly Fast at Debate', *USA Today*, 4 March 2016 (accessed August 20, 2016 from http://www.pressreader.com/usa/usa-today-us-edition/20160304/281513635242980).

Jenkins, J. (2000) *The Phonology of English as an International Language: New Models, New Norms, New Goals* (Oxford: Oxford University Press).

Jenkins, J. (2002) 'A Sociolinguistically Based, Empirically Researched Pronunciation Syllabus for English as an International Language', *Applied Linguistics*, 23(1), 83–103.

Jenkins, J. (2007) *English as a Lingua Franca: Attitude and Identity* (Oxford and New York: Oxford University Press).

Kachru, B. (1985) 'Standards, Codification and Sociolinguistic Realism: The English Language in the Outer Circle', in R. Quirk and H. Widdowson (eds) *English in the World: Teaching and Learning the Language and Literatures* (Cambridge: Cambridge University Press), pp. 11–30.

Kachru, B. (2006) 'English: World Englishes', in E. K. Brown and S. Ogilvie (eds) *Concise Encyclopedia of Languages of the World* (Amsterdam: Elsevier).

Kachru, Y. and L. E. Smith (2008) *Cultures, Contexts and World Englishes* (New York: Routledge).

Kenworthy, J. (1987) *Teaching English Pronunciation* (New York: Longman).

Krause, C. A. (1916) *The Direct Method in Modern Languages: Contributions to Methods and Didactics in Modern Languages* (New York: C. Scribner's Sons).

Kuo, I.-C. V. (2006) 'Addressing the Issue of Teaching English as a Lingua Franca', *ELT Journal*, 60(3), 213–21.

Labov, W. (1966) *The Social Stratification of English in New York City* (Washington, DC: Center for Applied Linguistics).

Lado, R. (1957) *Linguistics across cultures: Applied linguistics for language teachers*. Ann Arbor, MI: University of Michigan Press.

Larsen-Freeman, D. and M. Anderson (2013) *Techniques and Principles in Language Teaching*, 3rd edn (London: Oxford University Press).

Levis, J. M. (2006) 'Pronunciation and the Assessment of Spoken Language', in R. Hughes (ed.) *Spoken English, TESOL and Applied Linguistics* (London: Palgrave Macmillan), pp. 245–70 (accessed August 20, 2016 from http://link.springer.com/chapter/10.1007/978-0-230-58458-7_11).

Magrath, D. (2016) Applying linguistic theory to lesson production. *TESOL English Language Bulletin*, 12 August 2016 (accessed from http://exclusive.multibriefs.com/content/interference-patterns-applying-linguistic-theory-to-lesson-production/education)

McKay, S. L. (2002) *Teaching English as an International Language: Rethinking Goals and Approaches* (Oxford: Oxford University Press).

Morley, J. (1991) 'The Pronunciation Component in Teaching English to Speakers of Other Languages', *TESOL Quarterly*, 25(3), 481–520.

Nagata, N. (1993) 'Intelligent Computer Feedback for Second Language Instruction', *The Modern Language Journal*, 77(3), 330–39.

Official Rosetta Stone (2016) (accessed 8 March 2016 from http://www.rosettastone.com/).

Petrić, B. (2009) '"I Thought I Was an Easterner; It Turns Out I Am a Westerner!"': EIL Migrant Teacher Identities', in F. Sharifan (ed.) *English as an International Language: Perspectives and Pedagogical Issues* (Bristol, UK: Multilingual Matters), pp. 135–50.

Pulgram, E. (ed.) (1954) *Applied linguistics in language teaching*. Washington, DC: Georgetown University Press.

Purcell, E. T. and R. W. Suter (1980) 'Predictors of Pronunciation Accuracy: A Reexamination', *Language Learning*, 30(2), 271–87.

Rabecq, M. M. (1957) 'Comenius: Apostle of Modern Education', *Courier*, 11, 4–15.

Rahman, J. (2008) 'Middle-Class African Americans: Reactions and Attitudes toward African American English', *American Speech*, 83(2), 141–76, http://doi.org/10.1215/00031283-2008-009.

Rassias Foundation (1975) *The Rassias Language Method: Manual for Prospective Adopters* (Norwich, VT: Rassias Foundation).

Reed, M. and J. Levis (2015) *The Handbook of English Pronunciation* (Kindle Edition) (New York: Wiley).

Richards, J. C. (2013) 'Difference between an Approach and a Method?' Jack C. Richards: The Official Website of Educator & Arts Patron Jack C. Richards (accessed 8 March 2016 from http://www.professorjackrichards.com/difference-between-an-approach-and-a-method/).

Richards, J. C. and T. S. Rodgers (2015) *Approaches and Methods in Language Teaching* (Cambridge: Cambridge University Press).

Roach, P. (1998) 'Some Languages Are Spoken More Quickly Than Others', in L. Bauer and P. Trudgill (eds) *Language Myths* (London: Penguin Books), pp. 150–8 (accessed August 20, 2016 from http://www.personal.rdg.ac.uk/~llsroach/phon2/tempopr.htm).

Rogerson-Revell, P. (2011) *English Phonology and Pronunciation Teaching* (London: Bloomsbury Publishing).

Seidlhofer, B. (2005) 'English as a Lingua Franca', *ELT Journal*, 59(4), 339.

Selinker, L. (1972) 'Interlanguage', *International Review of Applied Linguistics in Language Teaching*, 10(3), 209.

Selivan, L. (2016) *Seventh International ETAI Conference Program Book*. Ashkelon, Israel, July 4–6, 2016.

Shaw, B. (1913) *Pygmalion: A Romance in Five Acts* (New York: Penguin Books).

Sung, C. C. M. (2013) '"I Would Like to Sound like Heidi Klum": What Do Non-native Speakers Say about Who They Want to Sound Like?', *English Today*, 29(2), 17.

Święciński, R. (2006) 'Teaching English Articulatory Settings Features to Polish Students of English – A Study of Phonation', *Dydaktyka Fonetyki Języka Obcego W Polsce*, 203–15.

Szpyra-Kozłowska, J. (2014) *Pronunciation in EFL instruction: A Research-based Approach* (Bristol, UK: Multilingual Matters).

Taylor de Caballero, K. (2015) 'Pronunciation Perspectives: A Video Conversation with Tracey Derwing', TESOL International Association, 14 August (accessed August 20, 2016 from http://blog.tesol.org/pronunciation-perspectives-a-video-conversation-with-tracey-derwing/).

Thomson, R. I. (2012) 'Accent Reduction', The Encyclopedia of Applied Linguistics, 5 November (accessed August 20, 2016 from http://onlinelibrary.wiley.com/doi/10.1002/9781405198431.wbeal0004/full).

Thomson, R. I. (2014) 'Myth 6: Accent Reduction and Pronunciation Instruction Are the Same Thing', in L. J. Grant (ed.) *Pronunciation Myths: Applying Second Language Research to Classroom Teaching* (Ann Arbor: University of Michigan Press), pp. 160–87.

Trofimovich, P. and W. Baker (2007) 'Learning Prosody and Fluency Characteristics of Second Language Speech: The Effect of Experience on Child Learners' Acquisition of Five Suprasegmentals', *Applied Psycholinguistics*, 28(2), 251–76.

Van Rooten, L. d'Antin (1980) *Mots d'heures, gousses, rames: the d'Antin manuscript* (New York: Penguin Books).

Wang, X. (2012) 'Auditory and Visual Training on Mandarin Tones: A Pilot Study on Phrases and Sentences', *International Journal of Computer-Assisted Language Learning and Teaching (IJCALLT)*, 2(2), 16–29.

Index

A

AAVE *See* African-American Vernacular English
accent   1, 2, 3, 4, 5, 6, 7, 13, 17, 31, 32, 39, 42, 43, 44, 48, 59, 63, 64, 66, 68, 69, 75, 82, 91,95, 110, 113, 116, 120, 121, 122, 123, 124, 130, 141, 148, 149, 154, 155, 156, 159, 160, 161, 165, 167, 175, 177, 182, 183, 186, 187, 191, 192
accent modification   124, 186
accent reduction *See* accent modification
affricate   41, 42, 48, 186
African-American Vernacular English   156
allophone   74, 85, 86, 87, 88, 89, 91, 92, 93, 96, 99, 110, 127, 129, 139, 180, 186
ALM *See* Audio-lingual Method
alveolar   7, 21, 29, 30, 31, 32, 33, 35, 41, 48, 186, 188
alveopalatal   32, 33, 34, 41, 48, 186
approximant   42, 44, 48, 186, 187, 191
Arabic   26, 42, 84, 104, 113, 122, 143, 157, 182
articulatory setting   32, 142, 143, 152, 187
ash   57, 58, 59, 60,61,67, 83
aspiration   31, 86, 89, 91, 92, 129, 141, 162, 187
assimilation   130, 133, 135, 182, 187
asterisk   53, 93
Audio-lingual Method   8, 109, 110, 112, 114, 115, 151, 170, 172, 173, 187

B

backward build-up   110, 111, 151
behaviourist   109, 173
bilabial   21, 22, 23, 24, 37, 48, 77
Black American English *See* African-American Vernacular English
broad transcription   69, 187, 191

C

CALL *See* Computer Assisted Language Learning
Canada   12, 48, 72, 158, 159
Cantonese   92, 109, 128
cap   32, 34
carry-over   124
CBI *See* Content-Based Instruction
cedilla   36
checked   53, 54
Chinese   4, 5, 94, 97, 98, 109, 116, 128, 142, 151, 157, 171
choral response   151
CLT *See* Communicative Language Teaching
cluster   34, 93, 97, 98, 128, 133, 162, 187
Cognitive Code Learning   173
Coleman report   108, 168
Comenius   104, 171, 187
Communicative Approach   112, 113, 114, 115, 120, 122, 158, 160, 170, 173
Communicative Language Teaching   112, 113, 114, 115, 120, 122, 158, 160, 170, 173
Community Language Learning   173
complementary distribution   93, 187

comprehensibility 120, 121, 124, 152, 160, 165, 169
comprehensible input 8, 187, 190
Computer Assisted Language Learning 116, 168, 174
Content-Based Instruction 173
contrastive analysis 110
contrastive distribution 93
Critical Age Hypothesis 81, 187
Critical Period Hypothesis *See* Critical Age Hypothesis
Czech 32, 41, 47, 60, 75, 83, 96, 109, 128, 130, 133, 136, 138, 146, 150, 187, 188

D
Danish 30
deep structure 76, 94, 188, 193
de-rhotacization 45
descriptive 38, 51, 158, 188, 192, 196
diaeresis 70, 188, 193
digraph 27, 32, 38, 41, 80, 188
diphthong 12, 68, 69, 70, 71, 77, 134, 135, 138, 188, 191, 194
Direct Method 106, 107, 108, 109, 172
Dominican Republic 11
Dutch 31, 57, 91, 130

E
EFL *See* English as a Foreign Language
EIL *See* English as an International Language
ELF *See* English as a Lingua Franca
ELT *See* English Language Teaching
English as a Foreign Language 102, 121, 152, 154, 160, 162, 164, 165, 166, 199
English as a Lingua Franca 3, 13, 154, 162, 163, 164, 166, 168, 188, 190
English as a Second Language 114, 165
English as an International Language 3, 161, 162, 163, 164, 165, 166, 188

English for Specific Purposes 9, 169, 174
English Language Teaching 13, 16, 101, 142, 160, 161, 162
ESL *See* English as Second Language
ESP *See* English for Specific Purposes
eth 28, 80
Expanding Circle 159

F
Farsi 97, 113
final devoicing 130, 133, 134, 188
flap 77, 139, 140, 141, 186, 188, 189, 193
flap D 139
fossilized 4, 112, 189
free variation 92, 189
French 6, 18, 20, 31, 34, 35, 36, 40, 41, 52, 56, 57, 61, 62, 69, 91, 93, 99, 105, 109, 110,147, 148, 154, 157, 163, 168, 172, 173, 186, 193
fricative 25, 26, 27, 28, 30, 33, 34, 35, 36, 40, 41, 42, 80, 84, 88, 90, 186
functional load 29, 60, 80, 122, 130, 189

G
German 20, 26, 31, 34, 36, 40, 41, 44, 46, 47, 52, 56, 57, 61, 62, 69, 84, 88, 98, 99, 105, 109, 110, 116, 117, 121, 130, 143, 155, 156, 157, 183, 186, 192
glide 45, 46, 66, 68, 69, 70, 189, 191, 194
glottal 40, 189
grammar translation 189
grammar-translation 104, 105, 106, 108, 109, 111, 171
Greek 27, 45, 60, 63, 66, 99, 105, 143
gum ridge *See* alveolar

H
Haitian Creole 118
hard palate *See* velum
Hebrew 11, 84, 105

Hindi 97
hypercorrection 47, 189, 190
hyperliteracy 16, 80, 190

I
Icelandic 26
identity 5, 12, 13, 124, 154, 164, 165
implosive 19
Indo-European 4
Inner Circle 159, 160, 161, 163
Input Hypothesis 190
intelligibility 5, 6, 7, 29, 39, 55, 61, 115, 119, 120, 121, 122, 124, 125, 133, 134, 138, 140, 150, 152, 160, 161, 162, 163, 164, 165, 167, 169, 171, 173, 182, 183, 184, 187, 190
interdental 26, 27, 28, 29, 48, 80, 190
International Phonetic Alphabet 7, 12, 16, 20, 22, 26, 27, 32, 34, 36, 44, 50, 54, 55, 56, 60, 65, 68, 71, 72, 87, 133, 138, 176, 178, 190
intervocalic 42, 139, 162, 186
intonation 9, 13, 127, 141, 145, 150, 151, 175, 190, 193
IPA *See* International Phonetic Alphabet
Irish 12, 120
Italian 54, 56, 57, 69, 148

J
Japanese 24, 94, 111, 113, 142, 147, 169

K
Korean 47

L
labial 21, 22, 23, 24, 37, 48, 77, 190
labiodental 24, 25, 26, 44, 47, 48, 190
labiovelar 46, 47, 190
langue 93
larynx 21, 23, 39, 189
lateral 43, 44, 45, 49, 190, 191

Latin 7, 26, 104, 105, 164, 171
lax 51, 53, 54, 55, 56, 57, 59, 60, 61, 62, 63, 64, 65, 66, 67, 90
lexical 36, 137, 138, 139, 140, 148, 151, 190, 192
LFC *See* Lingua Franca Core
lightning drill 134, 135, 149, 190
Lingua Franca Core 161, 162, 190
linguistic exogamy 103, 191, 197
liquid 42, 43, 44, 45, 48, 186, 190, 191
Lithuanian 32

M
manner of articulation 21, 22, 24, 30, 48, 90
minimal pair 6, 22, 23, 25, 28, 30, 35, 38, 39, 40, 53, 64, 70, 79, 80, 81, 82, 96, 191
motivation 3, 4, 108, 110, 113, 124, 160

N
narrow transcription 187, 191
nasal 24, 25, 26, 30, 31, 35, 37, 38, 48, 96, 110, 172, 191
natural class 62, 64, 89, 90
needs analysis 8, 9, 126, 169, 170, 181, 191
NNEST *See* non-native English-speaking teachers
non-native English-speaking teachers 162, 165
non-rhotic 161, 162, 192
Norwegian 30, 47

O
off-glide 45, 66, 68, 69, 70, 191, 194
Old English 33, 95, 155
open O 63, 64
orthography 17, 20, 26, 27, 28, 37, 52, 54, 58, 74, 135, 193
Outer Circle 159, 197

P
palatal 32, 33, 34, 36, 41, 46, 48, 186
parole 93, 191

Parsley Massacre 11
PAY 8, 9, 26, 30, 42, 102, 103, 104,
    105, 107, 108, 109, 111, 117,
    118, 119, 120, 122, 123, 124,
    125, 126, 131, 135, 139, 140,
    143, 149, 150, 152, 156, 158,
    170, 179, 181, 183, 185, 191
Persian 97
phoneme four, 74, 78, 79, 80, 81,
    82, 83, 84, 85, 86, 87, 88, 89, 90,
    91, 92, 93, 94, 96, 98, 99, 101,
    110, 111, 127, 129, 139, 155,
    170, 172, 176, 180, 186, 187,
    189, 191
phonemic 45, 72, 74, 79, 80, 81, 82,
    83, 85, 86, 87, 92, 94, 122, 133,
    134, 176, 188, 191
phonemic inventory 82, 83, 191
phonetics 1, 11, 12, 14, 16-73, 74,
    75, 76, 77, 78, 82, 99, 106, 150,
    167, 178, 180, 191
  acoustic phonetics 16, 187
  articulatory phonetics 12, 19, 187
  auditory phonetics 19, 187
phonology 1, 12, 13, 74-100, 161,
    167, 180, 191
phonotactic(s) 33, 34, 35, 36, 443,
    46, 48, 53, 59, 74, 85, 93, 94, 95,
    97, 98, 99, 104, 127, 128, 129,
    131, 133, 180, 191
pidgin language 103, 104
place of articulation 21, 22, 24, 37,
    39
Polish 7, 41, 43, 47, 136, 188, 199
Portuguese 36
prescriptive 38, 51, 188, 191
prosody 9, 13, 127, 138, 152, 153,
    173, 175, 180, 192
prosody pyramid 152, 153
prosthesis 97, 192

R
raspberry 76, 77, 78
Rassias Method 117, 192
Received Pronunciation 44, 159,
    160, 161, 192

relic 46, 52, 136
retroflex 44, 45, 192
rhotacized 66, 67
rhotic 45, 161, 162, 191, 192
rounded 51, 52, 55, 56, 57, 58, 60,
    61, 62, 63, 64, 65, 67, 90
RP *See* Received Pronunciation
Russian 35, 40, 84, 117, 136, 188,
    192

S
SAE *See* Standard American English
Sanskrit 104, 171
schwa 65, 66, 147
Second Language Acquisition 13,
    74, 104
semivowel 42, 46, 47, 48, 95, 186
Shakespeare 44, 148, 161
Shaw 12, 18
shibboleth 11, 12, 122, 192
shwa *See* schwa
Silent Way 173
SLA *See* Second Language Acquisition
Slavic 188
Slovak 6, 188
soft palate *See* velum
Spanish 6, 18, 24, 59, 60, 69, 84,
    91, 92, 93, 97, 109, 111, 112,
    123, 143, 189, 193, 194
Standard American English 6, 24,
    48, 50, 63, 160, 161
stop 9, 22, 24, 25, 26, 30, 35, 36, 37,
    38, 41, 42, 48, 84, 85, 86, 87, 89,
    90, 153, 173, 182, 186, 187, 189,
    191, 192
stress 9, 13, 53, 54, 59, 65, 66, 69,
    87, 127, 133, 136, 137, 138, 139,
    140, 141, 143, 144, 145, 146,
    147, 148, 149, 150, 151, 152, 162,
    170, 175, 186, 188, 190, 192, 193
stress-timed 147, 150, 192, 193
substitution drill 111
suffix 17, 18, 78, 131, 137
Suggestopedia 173
suprasegmental 9, 13, 101, 127-153,
    162, 172, 192, 193

surface structure   76, 94, 188, 193
Swedish   19, 30
syllabic   138
syllable-timed   147, 150, 193

T
tajweed   104
Task-Based Language Teaching   173
TBLT *See* Task-Based Language Teaching
teachable moment   112
tense   51, 53, 54, 55, 56, 57, 59, 60, 61, 62, 63, 64, 65, 67, 68, 69, 90, 190, 193
Thai   92, 113, 143
tone   4, 5, 13, 92, 109, 116, 127, 128, 168, 177, 193
Total Physical Response   173, 193
TPR *See* Total Physical Response
Tukano   103, 197

U
umlaut   52, 193
unrounded   51, 52, 55, 56, 57, 58, 60, 61, 62, 64, 65, 67, 90
uvula   7
uvular   44

V
Vedic   104
velar   37, 38, 40, 48, 84, 85, 86, 89, 96, 193

velum   7, 21, 35, 37, 38, 39, 46, 47, 190, 193
Vietnamese   19, 20
voiced   23, 25, 27, 28, 29, 30, 33, 34, 35, 37, 41, 44, 46, 48, 55, 69, 79, 80, 90, 130, 131, 132, 133, 134, 149, 162, 188, 189, 194
voiceless   23, 24, 25, 27, 28, 29, 30, 33, 34, 35, 36, 37, 40, 41, 55, 77, 80, 84, 85, 86, 89, 90, 131, 149, 162, 187, 189, 191, 194
voicing   21, 22, 23, 24, 25, 30, 31, 48, 90, 130, 133, 134, 188
vowel   12, 16, 17, 18, 22, 25, 28, 33, 38, 40, 41, 42, 45-73, 77, 79, 80, 87, 88, 90, 91, 92, 95, 97, 110, 28, 131, 132, 133, 134, 135, 137, 138, 139, 147, 150, 152, 162, 172, 186, 187, 188, 189, 191, 192, 193, 194
vowel chart   49, 62, 70
vowel purity   56, 194

W
wedge *See* cap
World Englishes   120, 122, 139, 159, 160, 162

Z
z   34

www.ingramcontent.com/pod-product-compliance
Lightning Source LLC
Chambersburg PA
CBHW052110300426
44116CB00010B/1605